Azure Resource Manager Templates Quick Start Guide

Create, deploy, and manage Azure resources with ARM templates using best practices

Ritesh Modi

BIRMINGHAM - MUMBAI

Azure Resource Manager Templates Quick Start Guide

Copyright © 2019 Packt Publishing

All rights reserved. No part of this book may be reproduced, stored in a retrieval system, or transmitted in any form or by any means, without the prior written permission of the publisher, except in the case of brief quotations embedded in critical articles or reviews.

Every effort has been made in the preparation of this book to ensure the accuracy of the information presented. However, the information contained in this book is sold without warranty, either express or implied. Neither the author, nor Packt Publishing or its dealers and distributors, will be held liable for any damages caused or alleged to have been caused directly or indirectly by this book.

Packt Publishing has endeavored to provide trademark information about all of the companies and products mentioned in this book by the appropriate use of capitals. However, Packt Publishing cannot guarantee the accuracy of this information.

Commissioning Editor: Vijin Boricha
Acquisition Editor: Shrilekha Inani
Content Development Editor: Kirk Dsouza
Technical Editor: Adya Anand
Copy Editor: Safis Editing
Project Coordinator: Hardik Bhinde
Proofreader: Safis Editing
Indexer: Tejal Daruwale Soni
Graphics: Alishon Mendonsa
Production Coordinator: Aparna Bhagat

First published: February 2019

Production reference: 1280219

Published by Packt Publishing Ltd.
Livery Place
35 Livery Street
Birmingham
B3 2PB, UK.

ISBN 978-1-78980-323-5

www.packtpub.com

`mapt.io`

Mapt is an online digital library that gives you full access to over 5,000 books and videos, as well as industry leading tools to help you plan your personal development and advance your career. For more information, please visit our website.

Why subscribe?

- Spend less time learning and more time coding with practical eBooks and Videos from over 4,000 industry professionals
- Improve your learning with Skill Plans built especially for you
- Get a free eBook or video every month
- Mapt is fully searchable
- Copy and paste, print, and bookmark content

Packt.com

Did you know that Packt offers eBook versions of every book published, with PDF and ePub files available? You can upgrade to the eBook version at `www.packt.com` and as a print book customer, you are entitled to a discount on the eBook copy. Get in touch with us at `customercare@packtpub.com` for more details.

At `www.packt.com`, you can also read a collection of free technical articles, sign up for a range of free newsletters, and receive exclusive discounts and offers on Packt books and eBooks.

Foreword

Azure Resource Manager is the control plane in Azure, and the global API that enables users from anywhere in the world to interact with their cloud resources, handling everything from authorization to throttling, auditing, policy, and template deployments.

Specifically as it relates to this book, Azure Resource Manager enables Infrastructure as Code in a declarative fashion for users to describe the goal state of their resources in Azure, regardless of whether they are complex end-to-end application architectures, or a complete deployment of the infrastructure topology.

This book focuses on the benefits of being Azure-Cloud-native with Azure Resource Manager and its templates, and through a practical approach, Ritesh demonstrates an ocean of benefits by using multiple different techniques to guide you to the desired outcome.

Kristian Nese

Azure Engineering

Contributors

About the author

Ritesh Modi is an ex-Microsoft Senior Technology Evangelist. He is a Microsoft Regional Director and the Regional Lead for Microsoft certified trainers.

He is an architect, senior evangelist, cloud architect, published author, speaker, and a known leader for his contributions to blockchain, Ethereum, data centers, Azure, bots, cognitive services, DevOps, artificial intelligence, and automation. He is the author of eight books.

He has spoken at more than 25 conferences, including TechEd and PowerShell Asia, and is a published author for MSDN magazine. He has more than a decade of experience of building and deploying enterprise solutions for customers. He has more than 25 technical certifications.

> *I have grown into a person who has more patience, perseverance, and tenacity while writing this book. I must thank the people who mean the world to me. I am talking about my mother, Bimla Modi, my wife, Sangeeta Modi, and my daughter, Avni Modi. I also thank Kirk Dsouza and the Packt team for their support.*

About the reviewer

Anindita Basak is a cloud architect and has been working with Microsoft Azure since its inception. With over a decade of experience, she helps enterprises to enable their digital transformation journey, powered by the cloud, DevOps, advanced analytics, and AI.

She co-authored *Stream Analytics with Microsoft Azure* and *Hands on machine Learning on Azure* from Packt Publishing, and was a technical reviewer of seven books on Azure. She has also authored two video courses on Azure Stream Analytics from Packt.

> *I'd like to thank my parents and brother for their unbounded support, and the Packt team!*

Packt is searching for authors like you

If you're interested in becoming an author for Packt, please visit `authors.packtpub.com` and apply today. We have worked with thousands of developers and tech professionals, just like you, to help them share their insight with the global tech community. You can make a general application, apply for a specific hot topic that we are recruiting an author for, or submit your own idea.

Table of Contents

Preface — 1

Section 1: Section 1: ARM Template Foundational Skills

Chapter 1: Infrastructure as Code and Configuration Management — 9
- What is configuration management? — 10
- Infrastructure as Code — 11
- What are ARM templates? — 13
- Designing ARM templates — 13
- A brief primer on JSON — 15
- Azure Resource Manager — 17
  - Provisioning — 17
    - Parallel — 19
    - Multi-region — 19
    - API-driven — 19
    - Automation — 19
  - Management — 19
    - Tags — 20
    - Resource groups — 20
    - Hierarchical — 20
  - Monitoring — 21
    - Logs — 21
    - Alerts — 21
    - Actions — 21
  - Governance — 22
    - Role-based access control — 22
    - Policies — 22
    - Locks — 23
- Summary — 23

Chapter 2: Azure Resource Manager Templates — 25
- Setting up the development environment — 26
  - Using Visual Studio 2017 as a development environment — 26
  - Using Visual Studio Code as a development environment — 28
- ARM template structure — 29
- Writing your first template — 31
- Template deployment — 35
  - Deployment using Azure portal — 36
  - Deployment using the Azure CLI — 39
  - Deployment using PowerShell — 40
    - Understanding Complete and Incremental deployment — 42

How does Incremental take care of these differences?	43
How to create and apply configuration in the case of Complete deployments	43

Parameters — 44
- Structure of a parameter in an ARM template — 44
- Referencing a parameter within a template — 46
- Grouping parameters — 47

Variables — 48
- Accessing variables — 49

Summary — 50

Chapter 3: Understanding Core Elements of ARM Templates — 51

ARM template expressions — 52
ARM template functions — 53
Resources — 54
- Resource names — 54
- Resource types — 55
- API Version — 55
- Resource properties — 57
- Resource locations — 58
- Resources and nested resources — 59
- Outputs — 59

A complete template — 60
Nesting resources — 61
Understanding dependsOn — 64
Using references — 67
Understanding resourceId — 72
Using linked templates — 75
Nested templates — 83
Summary — 85

Chapter 4: Advance Template Features — 87

Creating multiple instances of a resource type — 88
Creating multiple instances of a resource type, using Serial mode — 91
Creating multiple instances of a resource property — 92
Using copy to generate multiple variables — 94
Conditions in ARM templates — 97
- Conditions that return a Boolean value — 98
- Conditions that return condition values — 99

Advanced deployments — 101
- Using copy with deployment resources — 102
- Creating resource groups, using ARM templates — 103
- Deploying resources into multiple resource groups, using the deployment resource — 104
- Deploying resources into multiple resource groups in multiple subscriptions — 110
- Creating Nested Deployments — 112

Summary — 115

Section 2: Section 2: ARM Template Advanced Concepts

Chapter 5: IaaS Solutions Using Templates — 119
- Configuration inside an Azure virtual machine — 120
- Protecting scripts using SAS tokens — 125
- Using protectedSettings — 127
- CustomScriptExtension as separate resource — 129
  - Getting output from CustomScriptExtension — 131
  - Using CustomScriptExtension with Linux virtual machines — 132
  - Desired State Configuration — 134
  - Using configuration data — 137
- Summary — 140

Chapter 6: Unit Testing ARM Templates — 141
- Unit testing — 141
- Unit testing ARM templates — 142
- Retrieving outputs from ARM templates — 148
- Using Pester — 150
- Setting up the test harness — 151
  - Unit testing of a storage account — 152
  - Unit testing a public IP address — 152
  - Unit testing virtual networks — 153
  - Unit testing an NIC — 153
  - Unit testing a virtual machine — 155
  - The complete unit test script — 156
- Summary — 158

Chapter 7: Design Patterns — 159
- Why use modular ARM templates? — 159
  - Single responsibility principle — 160
  - Known configuration/T-shirt sizing — 160
- Scenario — 162
- Technical prerequisites — 163
  - Setting up Azure login and subscription — 163
  - New resource group — 163
  - Creating an Azure Storage Account — 164
  - Creating an Azure Storage blob container — 164
  - Generating an Azure Storage SAS token — 165
  - Uploading ARM templates to storage — 165
  - Creating an Azure Key Vault — 166
  - Creating secrets in Key Vault — 167
  - Creating the Azure AD Service Principal — 168
  - Assigning permissions to a Service Principal on Key Vault — 169
- Deploying the solution — 169

Table of Contents

Log to Azure using Service Principal	170
Deploying the ARM template	170
Template patterns	**171**
Modular ARM templates	172
Generalized templates	172
Azure SQL template	173
App service plan template	175
Azure App Services template	176
Using Key Vault for passwords and secrets	183
Static usage of Key Vault information	183
Dynamic declaration of Key Vault information	186
Dependencies between resources	188
Creating multiple resources in loop	190
Tagging of resources	192
Runtime sharing of property values	193
Redefining resources in the same template	**194**
Summary	**199**
Chapter 8: ARM Template Best Practices	**201**
Use resourceId function	**201**
Generate Resource Identifier used multiple times	**202**
Use Comments	**203**
Use Tags for resources and resource groups	**204**
Use parameters sparingly	**204**
Group related parameters	**205**
Order parameters alphabetically	**206**
Constraint parameters if possible	**206**
Parameter's defaultValue and API versions	**207**
Declare All Resources as top-level resources	**208**
Output Resource Properties and Configuration	**210**
Resource-naming conventions	**211**
Storage of Linked templates	**212**
Resource Dependencies	**212**
Using Key Vaults for secrets	**212**
Using ContentVersion	**212**
Deployment – Best Practices	**213**
Summary	**214**
Other Books You May Enjoy	**215**
Index	**219**

Preface

Azure Resource Manager (**ARM**) templates are the preferred, and possibly the best, way to implement **Infrastructure as Code** (**IaC**) for Azure Cloud. ARM templates also help you to implement effective DevOps, and the main goal of this book is to provide deeper insight into the concepts and implementation of ARM templates.

I spent a long time writing complex ARM templates while working at Microsoft, and continue to do so even now. This topic is quite close to my heart, and I just love writing ARM templates. I have gained so much knowledge on this subject that I thought of sharing it with others, and what better way to share than to write a book.

Who this book is for

This book is intended primarily for developers, DevOps engineers, and architects who have knowledge of Azure, but who also have little or no experience in planning and developing immutable infrastructure, comprising multiple Azure Services using IaC. Experienced professionals who have prior Azure knowledge also can benefit from this book, as it covers many areas of the Azure offering. This book also helps toward preparation for certifications.

What this book covers

Chapter 1, *Infrastructure as Code and Configuration Management*, starts by taking a look at configuration management and IaC. We will get introduced to the ARM framework provided by Azure, start to understand the concept of ARM templates, and learn the process of designing an ARM template. There is also a brief primer on JSON, since ARM templates themselves are based on JSON.

Chapter 2, *Azure Resource Manager Templates*, marks the start of our involvement with the development of ARM templates. We will start with the basics of ARM templates and cover the concepts that are essential for writing meaningful templates. This chapter will also include the usage of ARM template parameters and variables.

Chapter 3, *Understanding Core Elements of ARM Templates*, offers a detailed discussion of important ARM template concepts, including resources and outputs, and expressions and functions, along with a discussion on some of the most important functions, including reference and resourceId.

Chapter 4, *Advance Template Features*, covers real enterprise-level concepts, such as nested and linked templates, using deployment resources to invoke them, and using copy iterators to create multiple resources in sequence and parallel. We will also take a look at condition resources and learn about resource interdependency. This chapter also goes into a deeper implementation of cross-subscription, cross-resource group, and cross-region deployments using a single ARM template.

Chapter 5, *IaaS Solutions Using Templates*, focuses on exploring ARM templates for configuring environments using virtual machines. ARM templates provide virtual machine extensions that can automatically execute PowerShell and Desired State Configuration scripts following the creation of a virtual machine. This chapter will go deep into the trenches of these extensions, and provide solutions for both Windows and Linux operating systems.

Chapter 6, *Unit Testing ARM Templates*, covers topics on testing and maintaining the quality of ARM templates. We will investigate ways to unit test ARM template deployments and environments.

Chapter 7, *Design Patterns*, explores the composition of ARM templates that are modular, reusable, and maintainable. This chapter will provide a complete example for authoring an ARM template that is stored securely within Azure Storage blob containers, for storing credentials and secrets in Key Vaults, for provisioning and updating resources in the same ARM template, for linking and nesting templates, for autogenerating variables, and more.

Chapter 8, *ARM Template Best Practices*, focuses on using best practices while developing templates. These best practices help in creating ARM templates that are easy to change and maintain. They include parameters, variables, output and resource element best practices, security best practices, deployment-related best practices, and miscellaneous best practices.

To get the most out of this book

Readers will make the best use of this book if they first read the chapter and execute the code file associated with that chapter. Further knowledge may be acquired if readers go through the entire template, trying to understand the importance of each and every line of JSON code in each template. Finally, I would recommend that readers write these templates on their own at least once, so as to really develop complete hands-on knowledge of the subject. While doing so, you can refer to these templates as well.

Download the example code files

You can download the example code files for this book from your account at www.packt.com. If you purchased this book elsewhere, you can visit www.packt.com/support and register to have the files emailed directly to you.

You can download the code files by following these steps:

1. Log in or register at www.packt.com.
2. Select the **SUPPORT** tab.
3. Click on **Code Downloads & Errata**.
4. Enter the name of the book in the **Search** box and follow the onscreen instructions.

Once the file is downloaded, please make sure that you unzip or extract the folder using the latest version of:

- WinRAR/7-Zip for Windows
- Zipeg/iZip/UnRarX for Mac
- 7-Zip/PeaZip for Linux

The code bundle for the book is also hosted on GitHub at https://github.com/PacktPublishing/Azure-Resource-Manager-Templates-Quick-Start-Guide. In case there's an update to the code, it will be updated on the existing GitHub repository.

We also have other code bundles from our rich catalog of books and videos available at https://github.com/PacktPublishing/. Check them out!

Download the color images

We also provide a PDF file that has color images of the screenshots/diagrams used in this book. You can download it here: http://www.packtpub.com/sites/default/files/downloads/9781789803235_ColorImages.pdf.

Conventions used

There are a number of text conventions used throughout this book.

`CodeInText`: Indicates code words in text, database table names, folder names, filenames, file extensions, pathnames, dummy URLs, user input, and Twitter handles. Here is an example: "This function allows utilization of the value stored in `parameter` for any resource configuration. `parameters` can be referenced from the `variables`, `resources`, and `outputs` sections of the same template."

A block of code is set as follows:

```
"parameters": {
 "storageAccountName": {
 "type" : "string"
 }
}
```

When we wish to draw your attention to a particular part of a code block, the relevant lines or items are set in bold:

```
"[variables('multiLocation').location[copyIndex()].resourceGroupName]",
"properties": {
"mode": "Incremental",
"templateLink": {
"uri": "[variables('templateRefAppPlanTemplateUri')]",
"contentVersion": "1.0.0.0"
},
```

Any command-line input or output is written as follows:

```
Install-Module cmdlet
```

Bold: Indicates a new term, an important word, or words that you see on screen. For example, words in menus or dialog boxes appear in the text like this. Here is an example: "Provide a **Name** and **Location** in the **New Project** dialog box and click on **OK**."

Warnings or important notes appear like this.

Tips and tricks appear like this.

Get in touch

Feedback from our readers is always welcome.

General feedback: If you have questions about any aspect of this book, mention the book title in the subject of your message and email us at `customercare@packtpub.com`.

Errata: Although we have taken every care to ensure the accuracy of our content, mistakes do happen. If you have found a mistake in this book, we would be grateful if you would report this to us. Please visit `www.packt.com/submit-errata`, selecting your book, clicking on the Errata Submission Form link, and entering the details.

Piracy: If you come across any illegal copies of our works in any form on the internet, we would be grateful if you would provide us with the location address or website name. Please contact us at `copyright@packt.com` with a link to the material.

If you are interested in becoming an author: If there is a topic that you have expertise in, and you are interested in either writing or contributing to a book, please visit `authors.packtpub.com`.

Reviews

Please leave a review. Once you have read and used this book, why not leave a review on the site that you purchased it from? Potential readers can then see and use your unbiased opinion to make purchase decisions, we at Packt can understand what you think about our products, and our authors can see your feedback on their book. Thank you!

For more information about Packt, please visit `packt.com`.

Section 1: ARM Template Foundational Skills

In this section, the reader will learn the basics of ARM templates. This will include understanding important ARM template constructs and how to deploy them. Authoring complex templates using advanced features, including linked templates and nested templates, will also be part of this chapter. ARM templates have some unique features, such as functions and expressions, which will also be detailed in a comprehensive manner.

This section contains the following chapters:

- `Chapter 1`, *Infrastructure as Code and Configuration Management*
- `Chapter 2`, *Azure Resource Manager Templates*
- `Chapter 3`, *Understanding Core Elements of ARM Templates*
- `Chapter 4`, *Advance Template Features*

Infrastructure as Code and Configuration Management

Welcome, readers, to the world of Azure Cloud, **Azure Resource Manager (ARM)**, and ARM templates. Azure Cloud is growing in leaps and bounds and has good acceptability within enterprises. Azure Cloud provides a very performance-centric, scalable, and reliable Azure Resource Manager platform for management and governance of our deployments. To create resources on Azure, ARM templates are preferred over other mechanisms because of their inherent advantages. These advantages are mentioned throughout this book.

ARM templates have become an essential skill for any serious development on Azure, and writing reusable effective ARM template is sought after by many organizations. The Azure DevOps paradigm, to a large extent, also depends on ARM templates for its automation requirements.

In this first chapter, we will cover the following topics:

- Configuration management
- Infrastructure as code
- Understanding ARM templates
- Designing ARM template
- A primer on JSON
- Introducing Azure Resource Manager

What is configuration management?

Every deployment comprises two stacks of resources:

- Environment or infrastructure resources
- Application deployment

Infrastructure resources refer to hardware, software, and platform resources that make an environment suitable for application deployment. For example: infrastructure resources might contain hardware resources, such as networks, load balancers, network interface cards, physical server, virtual machines, network connectivity, an operating system, as well as platform resources, such as container runtime, and framework deployments, such as .NET core. Each of these infrastructure resources should be configured in a way that ensures the application will work according to its design.

After infrastructure resource-provisioning, the application is deployed on top of them. These are related to resources such as application binaries, application dependencies, and package installations.

The configuration of these resources is needed across environments—from higher-level environments, such as the production environment, to lower-level environments, such as the dev and test environments. There can be multiple environments for a solution. The configuration for each of these environments is different. The configuration for a production environment for a solution is different than the configuration of a development environment for the same solution. The configuration differences could be in terms of number of virtual machines, the size of virtual machines, the DNS names, the IP address range, and more. The application configuration for each of these environments is also different. For example: the connection string to database, integration endpoints to other systems, and other configurations are different across these environments.

Active management of both the infrastructure- and application-level configuration information as well as data is known as **configuration management** in software life cycle management parlance.

There are many tools that can help manage configurations across environments. Some of these are open source while others are propriety.

Each cloud provider also has its own configuration-management tools.

Azure provides ARM templates for provisioning and configuring the infrastructure resources. Other cloud vendors provide their own native ways to configure the environments.

Tools such as **Desired State Configuration**, **Chef**, **Puppet**, and **Ansible** are suitable for application configuration.

ARM templates enable a concept known as **Infrastructure as Code**; let's understand it in the next section.

Infrastructure as Code

Infrastructure as Code is one of the important facets of configuration-management systems. Generally, an environment is provisioned using manual efforts, such as using a self-service portal or wizard that provides step-by-step directions to configure a resource. It might go a step further and the environment can be provisioned using scripts, such as PowerShell and Bash. These scripts can then execute either manually or automatically using an orchestrator tool.

There are some serious limitations in using any of the previously mentioned approaches:

- Lack of repeatability, consistency, and predictability during provisioning and updating environments. The configuration values for scripts are either entered manually by copying from documents and Excel sheets.
- Lack of diagnostic information and it's difficult to figure out the exact error location.
- Human error while providing configuration values.
- Lack of confidence in deployments.
- Lack of efficiency and speed.

These limitations demand using a more systematic and automated approach for the creation of environments and the deployment of applications.

Infrastructure as Code can help remove these limitations. At a high level, Infrastructure as Code refers to the process of defining environments using code and then using it to create environments. However, Infrastructure as Code is much more than this. Infrastructure as Code mandates that infrastructure definitions after it's converted into code should follow the same application life cycle management principles that typically is followed for applications, they are as follows:

- They should be versioned and stored in a version-controlled repository. Developers should be able to author infrastructure-related code and push them into the repository.
- The repository helps with collaborating among developers about code related to infrastructure.

Infrastructure as Code and Configuration Management

- There should be a process established to verify and validate the changes done to infrastructure code to ensure that only well-tested code is deployed to higher-level environments.
- After verification, the code should be stored in a place that can be used by all the environments for creation and updates.
- Configuration information for each environment should be stored alongside the actual infrastructure code. These configurations can then be applied to each environment as applicable.
- After the infrastructure code is deployed to pre-production and production environments, appropriate operational validation should be conducted to ensure that the environment is behaving as intended and meeting expectations.
- There should be active monitoring of the environment and any deviation from the known desired configuration should be reported back.

The following screenshot is depicting the process followed for Infrastructure as Code:

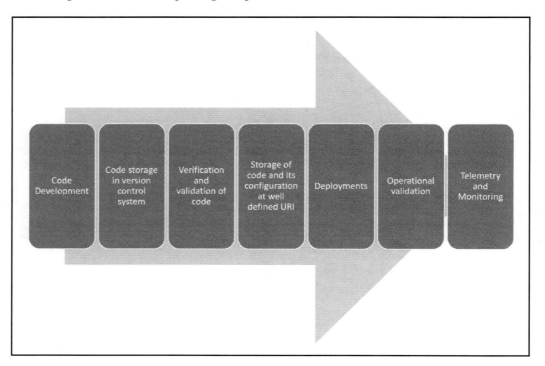

What are ARM templates?

ARM templates are JSON files and they enable Infrastructure as Code for Azure Cloud Platform. ARM templates help to provision and configure resources in a predictable, consistent, and repeatable manner.

ARM templates help in the following ways:

- Specifying resources and their configurations in a declarative manner. There is no scripting involved in provisioning resources.
- Providing intent and what should be provisioned by defining the resources rather than how to deploy the resources.
- Offers idempotent deployments by ensuring that the end state of the deployment is always consistent and predictable. This means that even during incremental deployments, the end state will remain consistent. It also means that templates deployed over and over will not change the end result, and environments will be equivalent when used to create multiple environments.
- Orchestrates the provisioning and configuration process by declaring dependencies between resources.
- Parameterizes the deployment process by enabling reusability, modular, and generic development.
- Cross-subscription, cross-region, and multiple resource group deployment and configuration of resources.
- Enables DevOps in the continuous integration and the continuous deployment of resources and the environment.

Designing ARM templates

ARM templates are one of the foundational pillars for the successful deployment of solutions on Azure. Authoring the right set of ARM templates—that are modular, reusable, and generic—is the first major task for ARM templates. The other aspect is the management and governance of these ARM templates. It is absolutely crucial to design the ARM template in a way that it can evolve over a period of time as well as be managed effectively.

The process for designing an ARM template is as follows:

- **Identification of resources**: This is the first step when designing ARM templates for a solution; it involves the identification of resources and their count. There are many resources that provide similar features; however, there are differences between them. It is advised to read the fine print of those resources before selecting them for the solution.
- **Resource location:** After resource identification, the location of these resources should be ascertained. Resources should be determined based on organizational policies and objectives. This also depends on sovereign rules and statutory regulations. The location is also determined based on the availability and pricing of resources in that region. There are also architectural requirements in terms of high availability, disaster-recovery, and performance to choose multiple locations for these resource locations.
- **Identification of the resource provider and its version**: Resources are made available in Azure by resource providers. Resource providers are containers that provide security and namespaces to resource types. Each resource provider provides an API layer through which clients interact with it. This API undergoes changes based on changes in the resource types it contains. If there are breaking changes in resources, the resource provider version is incremented to reflect the breaking changes. Also, the addition of new features will change the version number of these resource providers. These version numbers are based on the date on which they are released. While designing ARM templates, it is necessary to determine the appropriate resource-provider version number based on your requirements.
- **Sequencing**: Now that the Api version location and resources are identified, the sequence in which these resources should be provisioning needs to be determined. This is a necessary activity because a few resources might be dependent on other resources before they can be provisioned. This dependency could be because a resource might need data from other resources, or they could be a child resource of those resources.
- **Identification of parameters and variables**: Now that the sequencing of resources is determined, it is important to make the template generic, modular, and reusable. It is also important that templates are maintainable and easy to change. Parameters for resource configuration and the execution of templates should be ascertained such that templates can be reused across environments and solutions. Variables should be determined based on the number of times a value is used multiple times within the template.

- **Identification of output from the template**: The template output is important because it provides the return value and feedback about the execution of the template and its resources. This output also helps with testing the ARM templates.
- **Identification of the deployment process**: ARM templates can be deployed using Azure portal, Azure PowerShell, Azure CLI, REST API, and SDKs. It is important to identify the tools used for the deployment of ARM templates. Azure PowerShell and Azure CLI are preferred means for deploying ARM templates. Furthermore, an orchestrator tool, such as Azure DevOps should be used to automate the deployment process.

The preceding process is shown here:

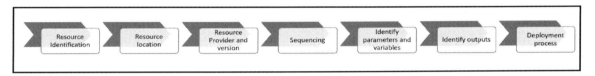

A brief primer on JSON

JavaScript Object Notation (JSON) is a lightweight data-representation and interchange format. It is a text-based and human-readable format that is easy to read, comprehend, and update. Many people think of JSON as a programming language or a markup language; however, it is neither. It is a pure representation of data in text format.

Prior to JSON, XML was the preferred data-exchange format and JSON has few similarities with it. Like XML, JSON is self-describing. It is quite easy to understand the intent of a JSON document by just reading through it. Also, like XML, it can create complex as well as nested objects. It is hierarchical, and objects can be composed of child objects and arrays. However, the similarities end here. JSON documents are terser and much more compact compared to XML documents. As a result, they are also much more reader-friendly. The data in XML documents is all string-based, however, in JSON, data can have types that make it easier to parse and validate them. The XML syntax is quite verbose compared to JSON.

JSON is supported by almost all programming languages and it provides SDKs to generate as well as read them intuitively.

There are a few limitations when it comes to JSON documents. They do not have any schema definition and documents do not have any fixed specification associated to them. In effect, there are no parsers or facilities to validate that a JSON document adheres to a certain specification.

A simple JSON document is shown here:

```
"customer" : {
            "customerId": 1,
            "firstName": "ritesh",
            "lastName": "Modi",
            "isRepeatCustomer": true,
            "address": {
                        "streetName": "10, Park Street",
                        "city": "Mumbai",
                        "Country": "India"
},
"productsOrdered": ["IPhone", "TShirt"]
}
```

Readers will notice that this JSON document is quite easy to read and comprehend. The basic JSON syntax comprises name-value pairs, where the name part is always decorated in double-quotes. Also, as a practice, the name part of the name-value pair follows the camel-casing naming standard. Each name is followed by a colon, `:`, and subsequently followed by the value part. Each name-value pair is separated using a comma: `,`.

A JSON document starts with a left curly bracket, `{`, and ends with a right curly bracket: `}`. A JSON value can hold values of numbers, strings, Boolean, objects, and array data types:

- **Strings**: Strings are a sequence of continuous characters and always enclosed within double quotes. In the preceding example, `India` is a string value assigned to `Country`. `"Country": "India"`; since double-quotes are special characters in JSON, they need to be escaped if they are part of the value. For example: `"/"India/""` will have an output of `"India"` assigned to the name element instead of just India without quotes.
- **Numbers**: JSON supports multiple data types related to numbers, including integers, scientific, and real numbers.
- **Boolean**: JSON supports true and false as Boolean values. They are never enclosed within quotes.
- **Null**: JSON also supports Null as a value. It means nothing is assigned to the name element.

- **Objects**: JSON also has a concept of an object. An object is a collection of key-value pairs enclosed within left curly brackets, `{`, and right curly brackets, `}`. Objects can be nested; that is, an object can contain another object as a child object. The `customer` document shown before in this section is an example of a JSON object.
- **Arrays:** JSON arrays start with left square brackets, `[`, and end with right square brackets, `]`. JSON arrays contain name-value pairs separated by a comma. They can also contain a set of values. `productsOrdered` in the previous example was an example of JSON arrays.

ARM templates support the following additional objects:

- **SecureString**: A secure string is similar to a native JSON string; the difference is that the ARM templates runtime ensures that these values are never written in log files. These values are not visible on the Azure portal. This datatype is used to pass credentials, keys, and secrets that should not be visible to anyone.
- **SecureObject**: A secure object is similar to native JSON arrays and objects. Again, these values are not visible in Azure portal and log files and are used to pass arrays and objects as secrets to ARM templates.

Azure Resource Manager

Azure Resource Manager, also popularly known as **ARM**, is the successor of Azure Service Management and is the new management framework that helps in provisioning, managing, monitoring, and governing Azure Resources.

Provisioning

The ARM framework helps to provision resources. The entire framework is highly scalable, performance-centric, and comprises multiple internal components. These components are not directly visible to users, but they help implement modularity and reusability within the overall architecture.

Here is the ARM architecture:

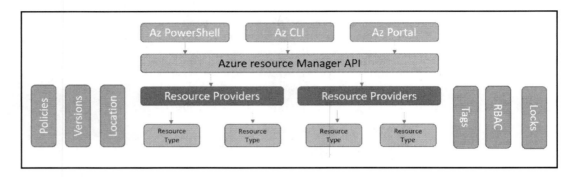

Here is the same architecture using examples of resource providers and types:

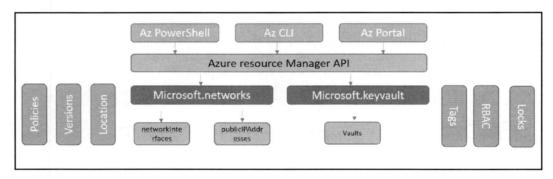

We will be referring to this architecture not only in this section but also throughout this chapter. The architecture comprises an **Azure Resource Manager API** component. This is one of the main components and the first point of contact with the Azure APIs for doing any operation within Azure. This is the control plane for the entire ARM framework.

When a client wants to talk to Azure, they must send their requests to this component. The ARM API does all the deciding, routing, and scheduling of resources. It hands over the incoming requests to other components that have designated responsibilities. While provisioning resources, it hands over the requests to the resource provider component, and the resource provider eventually ensures that resource instances are created based on the resource types controlled by them. Similarly, it hands over the request to other components, such as Azure policies, to evaluate the request and check whether the action in the request should be executed or denied.

Parallel

Resources are provisioned in Azure in parallel. This was one of the drawbacks of ASM. Resources were provisioned in sequence and that was a real productivity dampener, as well as less predictable from a deployment perspective. The ARM framework is built completely from scratch and ensures that resources can be provisioned in parallel. Users can provide their own dependency graph between resources while provisioning them.

Multi-region

The framework helps to provision resources in any Azure region where the resource provider and resource types are available. The request to provision a resource reaches the ARM API containing information about the target region and API ensures that it validates the configuration information and resource availability at a given location.

API-driven

The entire Azure framework is API-driven. There are various types of APIs, such as ARM, resource provider API, resource API, tenant API, usage API, cost API, and administrative API's. These APIs are scaled out automatically by Azure and are built using principles of single responsibility.

Automation

There are multiple types of clients that can interact with the ARM framework; the important ones are Azure PowerShell, the Azure command-line interface, Azure portal, ARM templates, Azure SDKs for different languages, and Azure REST APIs. These clients allow a varying degree of automation and implementation of DevOps.

Management

Cloud deployments need active management even more than on-premises deployment. The management of cloud resources refers to the organization of resources in a way that allows easy and faster appropriate report generation and provision of artifacts that can manage resources as a collection rather than individually.

Tags

ARM frameworks provide features to add metadata information to all resource types in every resource provider, including resource groups. This helps with designing a complete information-management repository for Azure Resources and with generating reports based on these tags. Tags can help generate cost and usage reports for different environments, departments, phases, services, products, and so on. The possibilities for such reports are endless as ARM allows the creation of custom tags.

Resource groups

Resource groups are logical containers for hosting resources in Azure. A resource cannot exist without being contained in a resource group. A resource group is a management container that provides security boundary, policy, and locks assignments, reporting on cost, usage, and logs related to management-plane activities. A resource group is created within a region; however, resources contained in it can be in a different location and need not be in the same location as a resource group. Resource groups help with managing multiple resources as a group.

Hierarchical

ARM framework manages access, authorization, policies, locks, and other management-related features in a hierarchical way. It means that there are parent-child relationships between these artifacts. The artifacts that form this hierarchy are management groups, subscriptions, resource groups, and resources. Providing access at the subscription level automatically provides access to the resource groups and the resources within them. The top most artifact is management group, which is a logical container for grouping Azure subscriptions; below it, subscriptions and resource groups are within subscriptions, and finally resources are within resource groups. This feature helps with the easy management and application of management-related activities to multiple subscription, resource groups, and resources.

Monitoring

The ARM framework provides monitoring capabilities for all its resources and resource groups. Monitoring helps to capture the essential telemetry and events. They store this data into storage accounts and other resources that are easily accessible, and then generate reports based on them. Azure provides numerous reports out of the box based on this data. Monitoring helps to identify issues with any resource related to health, performance, and availability. It also helps to identify changes made to the resources along with relevant information about initiator, date and time, activity performed, and other data.

Logs

Every resource in Azure generates events and telemetry that are logged in log files. The telemetry information is related to the health of the resource, including CPU utilization memory availability and network stats, and are written to the diagnostic logs. The events generated include any management control plane changes/updates/deletion of resources, and are written to the activity log. There are multiple types of log storage and these logs can be combined using log analytics.

Alerts

Azure provides features to generates alerts based on log data that's captured using monitoring. These alerts could be based on multiple events, and this typically involves the health of a resource. Custom alerts can be configured; based on them, appropriate actions can be initiated.

Actions

The alerts are defined based on rules and are generated once the log files identify data that meets the condition of these rules. An action can be automated to be executed based on these alerts. The actions include notifying stakeholders using email, text messages, or by calling them. It could also be configured to execute scripts in Azure functions or Azure automation runbooks.

Governance

Any enterprise cloud platform should provide enough governance features to manage deployments effectively. **Governance** refers to the exercising policies to control over deployment and access to resources and resource groups. It also means creating policies that meet the organizational objectives.

Role-based access control

After authenticating and gaining access to the Azure environment, there is an additional layer that checks for access authorization to the resource and resource group. This additional layer is **role-based access control** (**RBAC**), which checks whether the user who is trying to access the resource has permissions to access and perform the activity it intends to perform. It is composed of three different components:

- **Permissions**: Also known as **role definition**
- **Scope**: The scope on which the permissions are evaluated. They are resource groups and resources
- **Principal**: The actor trying to access the resources. It could be a user, group, or a service principle

RBAC assigns permissions to a principle at a given scope. For example, contributor permission is assigned to a service principal for a resource group.

It is also hierarchical and flows down from subscription to the resource group, and finally to the resource level.

Any permissions assigned to a principal at a resource group scope automatically gets the same access for resources contained within that resource group.

Policies

Policies is another important feature provided by the ARM framework. Policies provide control over the management plane of resources. While RBAC provides control on access to the data plane, Policies provides control over the management plane. It means that policies affect access and permissions to provision a resource. For example, a policy could explicitly deny the creation of resource in all regions apart from Central US and East US. These policies are checked while creating a new resource and are also evaluated for the existing resources.

Locks

Locks ensure that resources cannot be deleted or updated. This feature ensures that every ownership having permission on a scope, a principal cannot delete a resource. This is an additional layer of resource protection and especially useful for resources that are critical for working out a solution. The resources can only be deleted after removing the lock. There are two modes:

- **CanNotDelete**: This lock prevents deletion of a resource. Under this mode, resources can be updated and read at the management-control level.
- **ReadOnly**: This lock prevents deleting and updating a resource or resource group. This is more constraint compared to the CanNotDelete mode.

Summary

This chapter provided information about foundational concepts related to Azure Cloud, ARM, and ARM templates. Infrastructure as Code is a relatively new paradigm and should be adopted by enterprises to automate the process of provisioning environments. They also help in making Azure DevOps effective and efficient. ARM templates help to provision environments using a declarative approach. This helps to define the environment using JSON language and provides numerous ways to deploy them.

ARM provides an extensible and performant framework to manage, provision, and govern resources. We covered these topics in detail and provided a basic primer on JSON – the language of ARM templates.

We will start exploring ARM templates in more detail from the next chapter onward, and will cover the tools needed to create, deploy, and write basic ARM templates.

2
Azure Resource Manager Templates

This is where we will start getting involved with the development of **Azure Resource Manager** (**ARM**) templates. All subsequent chapters will add additional concepts or enhance the concepts discussed in this chapter. As we know, ARM templates are configurations written as code and go through the same development life cycle as an application. ARM templates use JSON to declare Azure resources and their configuration. Although ARM templates are based on JSON, there are specific syntaxes, nuances, and grammar that needs to be followed for successful authoring and deployment.

In this chapter, we will start with the basics of ARM template and cover the high-level concepts that are essential for any ARM template.

In this chapter we will cover the following topics:

- Setting up development the environment for ARM templates
- Structure of ARM templates
- Creating your first ARM template
- Exploring different ways to deploy ARM templates on Azure
- Understanding and implementing parameters and variables

Although ARM templates are JSON-based and JSON can be written in plaintext using any text editor, to be more productive, it is important that a development environment or a development editor is used. There are multiple editors available that support the development of ARM templates; prominent among them is Visual Studio.

Setting up the development environment

In this section, we will set up our development environment so that it can be used throughout this book. As mentioned, Visual Studio is the most prominent development editor for ARM templates. Visual Studio comes in multiple SKUs and flavors. Developing ARM templates can be performed using Visual Studio as well as Visual Code. Although Visual Studio provides boilerplate PowerShell code for the deployment of ARM templates as well as scaffolding code for some of the widely-used resources, it is also fast and easy to get started with the development activities.

Using Visual Studio 2017 as a development environment

Visual Studio comes in multiple SKUs, such as professional, enterprise, and community, and developing ARM templates can be done using the SKU you like best. Moreover, there are multiple versions of Visual Studio—the current prominent ones are Visual Studio 2015 and 2017. Since Visual Studio 2017 is the most updated and loaded environment, we will use it to create the development environment.

Visual Studio can be downloaded and installed from `https://visualstudio.microsoft.com/downloads/`. I am not showing the steps of installing Visual Studio, but it is important that the Azure SDK is deployed along with it. Visual Studio is based on modular component deployment and readers can customize the deployment based on their development needs. It is important that the **Azure development** workload is chosen when deploying Visual Studio 2017. If Visual Studio 2017 is already deployed, the **Azure development** workload can be deployed by modifying the installer configuration:

Chapter 2

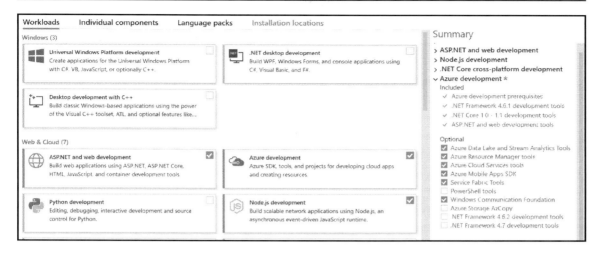

Once Visual Studio 2017 is deployed, it should have ARM templates available as part of the project templates:

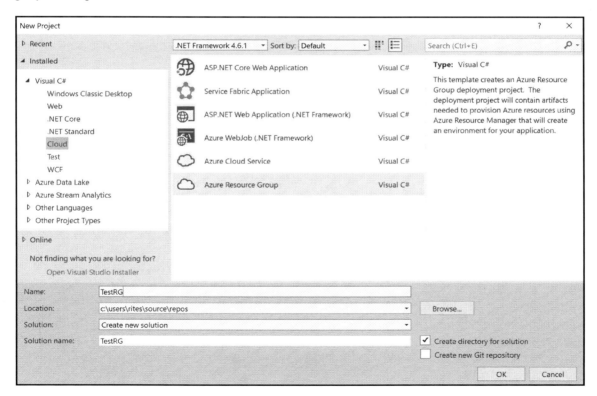

Using Visual Studio Code as a development environment

Visual Studio Code is lightweight development environment that supports cross-platform, open source development seamlessly. Visual Studio Code can be downloaded from the same location as Visual Studio 2017. ARM templates files, the Azure SDK, and PowerShell modules are not automatically installed as these were with Visual Studio Azure development module; they need to be downloaded and installed separately.

Azure PowerShell modules can be installed manually by downloading them from https://azure.microsoft.com/en-in/downloads/. They can also be installed using the PowerShellGet module if you are using PowerShell 5.0 or newer. The command for installing Azure PowerShell module using PowerShellGet is Install-Module -Name AzureRM.

The Azure ARM template extension can be installed in Visual Studio Code using the following steps:

1. Open the extensions pane in Visual Studio Code by pressing *Ctrl + Shift + X*
2. Type Azure Resource Manager Tools and click on the **Install** button:

It will take few seconds to install the ARM template development extension. This extension provides IntelliSense and other developer productivity features.

For this book, we will use Visual Studio 2017 to create our first ARM template; however, before writing our first ARM template, it's good to understand the overall structure of an ARM template.

ARM template structure

ARM templates have six top-level elements:

- `schema`
- `contentVersion`
- `parameters`
- `variables`
- `resources`
- `outputs`

Here's a typical template without any meaningful data:

```
{
    "$schema": "http://schema.management.azure.com/schemas/2015-01-01/deploymentTemplate.json#",
    "contentVersion": "1.0.0.0",
    "parameters": {
    },
    "variables": {
    },
    "resources": [
    ],
    "outputs": {
    }
}
```

Let's take a look at each of these elements:

- `schema`: Defines the grammar, scope, and constraints for elements that are legal and can be used within the template. It helps to ensure that only elements that will keep the template well-defined and valid are allowed, otherwise it will generate an error. The `schema` also provides the structure for complete ARM templates, including all resources. The value for the schema is an URI that can be navigated to and it is collection of Resource schema URI's. Each resource has its own `schema` and they all are referred as sub-schemas. One example is a schema for a virtual machine. The schema for virtual machines is defined at `https://schema.management.azure.com/schemas/2017-07-01-preview/CloudSimple.PrivateCloudIaaS.json#/resourceDefinitions/virtualMachines`, and this URI is mentioned within the master `schema` URI. It is mandatory to have this section in ARM templates.

- `contentVersion`: Provides a means of assigning the version number to the template. A template can evolve over time due to feature enhancements or bug fixes. `contentVersion` helps in creating multiple versions of the same template. This is similar to version control for code using Azure DevOps or GitHub. For ARM templates, a four-part string identifier acts as version number. `contentVersion` is used while having parent-child relationship between linked templates. We will go through the linked template in Chapter 3, *Understanding Core Elements of ARM Templates*, of this book. It is mandatory to have this section in ARM templates.
- `parameters`: This section provides us with the capability to accept values from users and help customize the template. It helps to increase the overall reusability of the template. We will look at parameters in greater detail in the *Parameters* section of this chapter. The `parameters` section accepts a JSON object as its value. This JSON object can contain multiple parameter definitions.
- `variables`: Provides ability to define a value once and reuse it multiple times within the template. This helps in writing maintainable and bug-free templates. Again, we will look at variables in the *Variables* section. The `variables` section accepts a JSON object as its value. This JSON object can contain multiple variable definitions.
- `resources`: This section is the core and main element of an ARM template. It is an optional element in the template structure. All resources and their configurations are declaratively defined here. When an ARM template is deployed, the `resources` section creates defined resources and configures them according to given specifications. Almost all of the chapters will focus on resources section to a great extent. The `resources` section accepts a JSON array as its value. This JSON array can contain multiple resource definitions. Square brackets, `[]`, in JSON denote an array, while curly brackets, `{}`, denote a JSON object.
- `outputs`: This section provides the ability to return or output values from templates to the user. This helps in finding the status of template execution and getting valuable information that is otherwise difficult to find and navigate. Chapter 3, *Understanding Core Elements of ARM Templates*, discusses `outputs` in greater detail. The `objects` section accepts a JSON object as its value. This JSON object can contain multiple output definitions.

The preceding template structure cannot be deployed because it does not have resources defined within the mandatory `resources` section. At least one resource should be defined for a template to be deployable.

Writing your first template

Now it's time to focus and create our first ARM template using Visual Studio 2017. Open Visual Studio 2017 and select **File** | **New** | **Project** | **Cloud** | **Azure Resource Group**. Provide a **Name** and **Location** in **New Project** dialog box and click on **OK**:

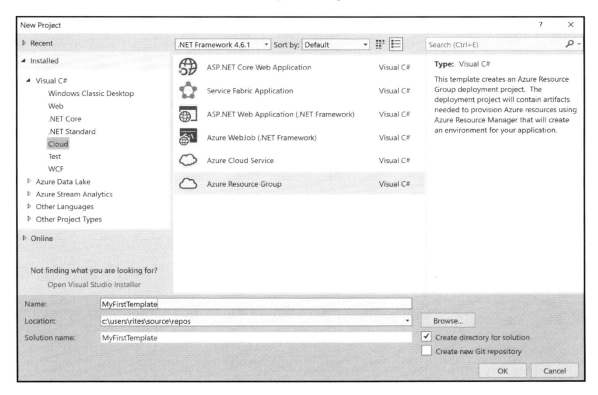

Select **Blank Template** and click on **OK**:

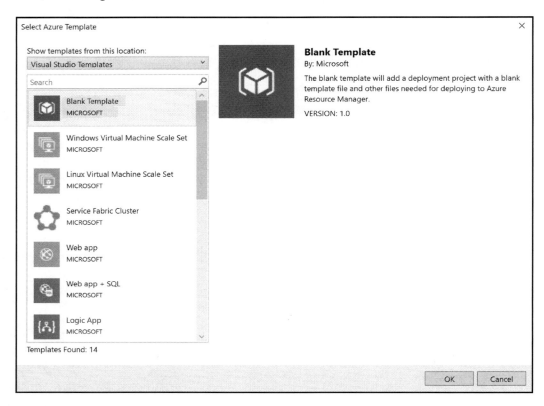

This should create a solution and the MyFirstTemplate project in Visual Studio. It will also create an ARM template file named azureDeploy.json and a template parameters file named azureDeploy.parameters.json. There is also a PowerShell file, Deploy-AzureResourceGroup.ps1, for both creating a resource group and deploying a template in it. We are not going to use it. Readers can go ahead and delete it:

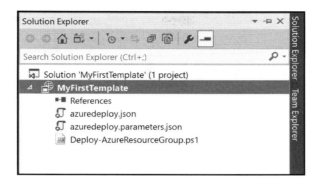

The content of the `azuredeploy.json` file is the same as shown before; for simplicity's sake, it is shown again:

```
{
  "$schema": "https://schema.management.azure.com/schemas/2015-01-01/deploymentTemplate.json#",
  "contentVersion": "1.0.0.0",
  "parameters": {},
  "variables": {},
  "resources": [],
  "outputs": {}
}
```

If readers try to deploy this template, it will successfully get deployed, however, it would not do anything meaningful at this stage.

Let's add a parameter, variable, resource, and an output to this template so it does something meaningful. It is possible that readers might not be able to understand many sections within this ARM template, but let me assure you that by the time you finish reading Chapter 5, *IaaS Solutions Using Templates*, everything will become crystal clear to you.

This template is responsible for provisioning a new storage account on Azure. The name of the storage account is available as a parameter, the SKU of the storage account is defined in the `variables` section, and the output consists of the storage name concatenated with the storage SKU.

Azure Resource Manager Templates

The entire code listing is shown here:

```json
{
    "$schema": "https://schema.management.azure.com/schemas/2015-01-01/deploymentTemplate.json#",
    "contentVersion": "1.0.0.0",
    "parameters": {
        "storageAccountName": {
            "type" : "string"
        }
    },
    "variables": {
        "storageType": "Standard_LRS"
    },
    "resources": [
        {
            "type": "Microsoft.Storage/storageAccounts",
            "name": "[parameters('storageAccountName')]",
            "apiVersion": "2018-02-01",
            "location": "[resourceGroup().location]",
            "sku": {
                "name": "[variables('storageType')]"
            },
            "kind": "Storage"
        }
    ],
    "outputs": {
        "storageDetails": {
            "type": "string",
            "value": "[concat(parameters('storageAccountName'), variables('storageType'))]"
        }
    }
}
```

Let's take a look at each of these elements:

- Line 2 declares the `schema` element.
- Line 3 defines the version of the template.
- Lines 4—8 define a single parameter named `storageAccountName` of the `string` type.

- Lines 9—11 define a single variable named `storageType` with the `Standard_LRS` value.
- Lines 12—23 define a single storage account resource within the resources array. The name for the resource gets its value from the parameters and syntax. `[parameters('storageAccountName')]` is an expression that is evaluated at runtime to get a value from the `storageAccountName` parameter. Similarly, the `[variables('storageType')]` syntax on line 19 is an expression that is evaluated at runtime to get a value from the `strorageType` variable. Line 17 has an expression that consists of an out-of-the-box ARM template function, `resourceGroup`, with the location as its property. It returns the Azure location for the resource group within which the resource is getting provisioned. ARM template expressions and functions will be covered in Chapter 3, *Understanding Core Elements of ARM Templates*.
- Lines 24—29 define the `outputs` section and it consist of single output named `storageDetails` of the `string` type. The value is generated at runtime using the `concat` function, which concatenates the `storageAccountName` parameter and the `strorageType` variable together.

Template deployment

A template can be deployed to Azure in multiple ways, including the following:

- Manually using the Azure portal
- Using the Azure CLI
- Using Azure PowerShell

There are other mechanisms, such as Azure Cloud Shell, .NET code, and the REST API, through which ARM templates can be deployed.

Deployment using Azure portal

Deploying a template using portal is quite straight forward. Log into your Azure portal and create a new **Resource groups** by providing the name and location, and then selecting an appropriate **Subscription**:

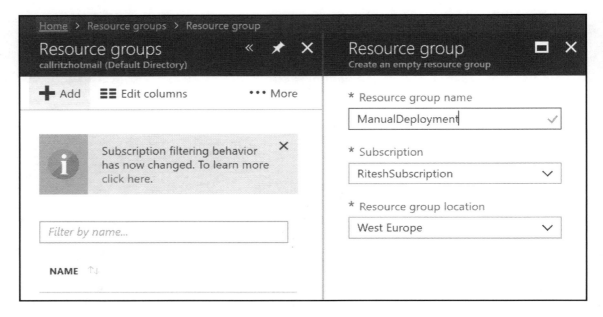

After creating **Resource group**, the template deployment resource should be selected and either a template can be imported from the existing GitHub repository or a template can be authored from portal itself. You can paste the ARM template code we created earlier in this editor and save it:

```
{
    "$schema": "https://schema.management.azure.com/schemas/2015-01-01/deploymentTemplate.json#",
    "contentVersion": "1.0.0.0",
    "parameters": {
        "storageAccountName": {
            "type" : "string"
        }
    },
    "variables": {
        "storageType": "Standard_LRS"
    },
    "resources": [
        {
            "type": "Microsoft.Storage/storageAccounts",
            "name": "[parameters('storageAccountName')]",
            "apiVersion": "2018-02-01",
            "location": "[resourceGroup().location]",
            "sku": {
                "name": "[variables('storageType')]"
            },
            "kind": "Storage"
        }
    ],
    "outputs": {
        "storageDetails": {
            "type": "string",
            "value": "[concat(parameters('storageAccountName'), variables('storageType'))]"
        }
    }
}
```

After saving, select an appropriate **Subscription**, the **Resource group** we just created, and provide the value for the **Storage Account Name** parameter, then click on **Purchase** to deploy the template. You will also have to agree to the terms and conditions before you can deploy the template:

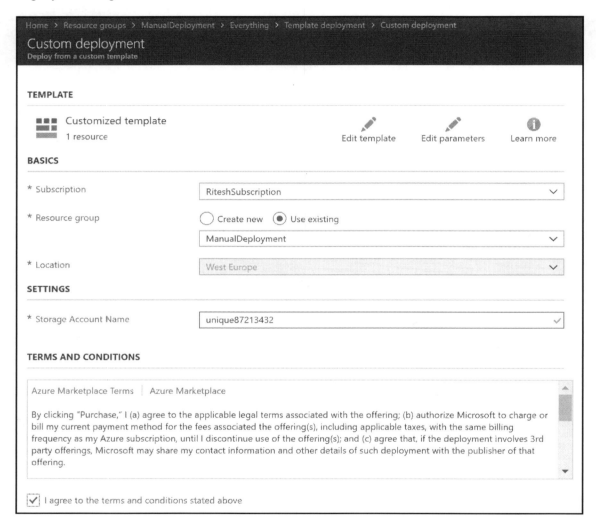

Deployment using the Azure CLI

The Azure CLI stands for command-line interface and helps to interface and automate resources in Azure across operating systems and programming languages. The Azure CLI must be installed before using it to deploy templates. To install the Azure CLI, please follow the steps at `https://docs.microsoft.com/en-us/cli/azure/install-azure-cli`.

Once the Azure CLI is installed, open the command prompt in Windows and run the following command:

```
Az login
```

This command generates a unique code that should be used with the URL provided by the same command. Clicking on **Continue** will prompt for your credentials. After successful authentication, you will see the following screen:

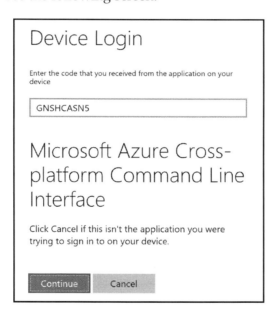

The command prompt will display all subscriptions the user is assigned.

Execute the following command on the command prompt to create a new **Resource group** named `CLIDeployment` in the `West Europe` location:

```
az group create --name CLIDeployment --location "West Europe"
```

The command runs as follows:

```
{
  "id": "/subscriptions/9755ffce-e94b-4332-9be8-1ade15e78909/resourceGroups/CLIDeployment",
  "location": "westeurope",
  "managedBy": null,
  "name": "CLIDeployment",
  "properties": {
    "provisioningState": "Succeeded"
  },
  "tags": null
}
```

Execute the following command to deploy our previously-authored template to the newly-created resource group:

```
az group deployment create --name CLIDeploy1 --resource-group CLIDeployment --template-file C:\Users\rites\source\repos\MyFirstTemplate\MyFirstTemplate\azuredeploy.json --parameters storageAccountName=unique824798
```

This should deploy the template and results in the following successful execution:

```
    ],
    "provisioningState": "Succeeded",
    "template": null,
    "templateLink": null,
    "timestamp": "2018-07-31T06:06:47.944369+00:00"
  },
  "resourceGroup": "CLIDeployment"
```

Deployment using PowerShell

PowerShell provides additional comments to check the validity of the templates before actual deployment.

The `Test-AzureRmResourceGroupDeployment` cmdlet can be used to test the validity of a template before deployment. Please note that this cmdlet cannot catch runtime configuration, naming, and dependency issues between resources; however, it will catch and report issues if there are syntax issues or if the grammar does not follow the rules of ARM templates. It is recommended to use this cmdlet before actual deployment:

```
Test-AzureRmResourceGroupDeployment -ResourceGroupName "TestRG" -Mode Incremental -TemplateFile "C:\myARMTemple.json" -TemplateParameterFile "C:\myARMTemplateParameters.json" -Verbose
```

`ResourceGroupName` is the name of the target resource group for deployment. `Mode` determines `Incremental` or `Complete` deployment, `TemplateFile` refers to the location of the ARM template on the local machine, `TemplateParameterFile` refers to the location of the ARM template parameters file, and it is good to use the `Verbose` switch to get more meaningful information of testing the deployment artifacts. It is mandatory to provide values for the `ResourceGroupName` and `TemplateFile` cmdlet parameters; the rest of them are optional.

You can deploy a template using the `New-AzureRmResourceGroupDeployment` cmdlet. This cmdlet has multiple property sets, which means that it can be used to deploy templates that are stored on a local machine, stored remotely on Azure Storage Account, or stored at any other location that can be referenced using HTTP URL. It supports both `Incremental` as well as `Complete` deployment. It also accepts parameters by way of the `parameters` file or by way of explicit parameters. The code listing shown next shows the command for deploying a template in incremental mode by supplying both the template and its `parameters` file:

```
New-AzureRmResourceGroupDeployment -Name "TestDeploy1" -ResourceGroupName
"TestRG" -Mode Incremental -TemplateFile "C:\myARMTemple.json" -
TemplateParameterFile "C:\myARMTemplateParameters.json" -Verbose
```

The `parameters` for a new cmdlet is almost like the `Test` cmdlet. The only difference is the addition of a new `Name` parameter and deployments are identified using this parameter.

It is important to note that a resource group must exist before a template can be deployed. This is because a template needs a resource group to be available as a prerequisite. Template deployment will not create a resource group automatically.

ARM template parameters can be explicitly provided with cmdlet. This cmdlet generates dynamic parameters for accepting these templates that is defined in parameters.

The script for deploying a template without a parameters file is shown next:

1. Create a new Resource group using the `New-AzureRmResourceGroup` cmdlet and providing the `Name` and `Location` of the Resource group. You should have been authenticated to Azure using the `Login-AzureRmAccount` cmdlet before running any of the following Azure PowerShell cmdlet:

```
PS C:\Users\rites> New-AzureRmResourceGroup -Name "FirstResourceGroup" -Location "East US"

ResourceGroupName : FirstResourceGroup
Location          : eastus
ProvisioningState : Succeeded
Tags              :
ResourceId        : /subscriptions/364c7779-65a1-4Ded-8847-c7a86661c1c3/resourceGroups/FirstResourceGroup
```

2. The template is tested for correctness using the `Test-AzureRmResourceGroupDeployment` cmdlet:

```
PS C:\Users\rites> Test-AzureRmResourceGroupDeployment -ResourceGroupName "FirstResourceGroup" -Mode Incremental -TemplateFile "c:\users\rites\source\repos\MyFirstTemplate\MyFirstTemplate\azuredeploy.json" -storageAccountName "unique9634name" -Verbose
VERBOSE: 8:55:28 AM - Template is valid.
```

3. The template is deployed using the `New-AzureRmResourceGroupDeployment` cmdlet:

```
PS C:\Users\rites> New-AzureRmResourceGroupDeployment -Name "FirstDeploy1" -ResourceGroupName "FirstResourceGroup" -Mode Incremental -TemplateFile "c:\users\rites\source\repos\MyFirstTemplate\MyFirstTemplate\azuredeploy.json" -storageAccountName "unique9634name" -Verbose
VERBOSE: Performing the operation "Creating Deployment" on target "FirstResourceGroup".
VERBOSE: 8:56:20 AM - Template is valid.
VERBOSE: 8:56:26 AM - Create template deployment 'FirstDeploy1'
VERBOSE: 8:56:26 AM - Checking deployment status in 5 seconds
VERBOSE: 8:56:33 AM - Checking deployment status in 5 seconds
VERBOSE: 8:56:39 AM - Resource Microsoft.Storage/storageAccounts 'unique9634name' provisioning status is running
VERBOSE: 8:56:39 AM - Checking deployment status in 13 seconds
VERBOSE: 8:56:54 AM - Checking deployment status in 5 seconds
VERBOSE: 8:57:00 AM - Checking deployment status in 5 seconds
VERBOSE: 8:57:06 AM - Resource Microsoft.Storage/storageAccounts 'unique9634name' provisioning status is succeeded


DeploymentName          : FirstDeploy1
ResourceGroupName       : FirstResourceGroup
ProvisioningState       : Succeeded
Timestamp               : 2018-07-30 12:57:04 PM
Mode                    : Incremental
TemplateLink            :
Parameters              :
                          Name                Type         Value
                          ==================  ===========  ==========
                          storageAccountName  String       unique9634name

Outputs                 :
                          Name                Type         Value
                          ==================  ===========  ==========
                          storageDetails      String       unique9634nameStandard_LRS

DeploymentDebugLogLevel :
```

An interesting aspect of this template deployment is that it outputs custom name-value pairs as defined within the `Outputs` section of the ARM template. The values of these are derived at runtime and returned to the caller.

Understanding Complete and Incremental deployment

We learned in `Chapter 1`, *Infrastructure as Code and Configuration Management*, that deployments should be consistent, predictable, and idempotent. This means that resources should always be in a deterministic state after deployment and the state should match the state mentioned within the template.

By default, ARM templates are Incremental in nature. What does Incremental mean in terms of deployment? It means that whatever resources are available in the template should also be available in Azure, and the resource configurations should match the configuration provided in the template. However, there are a few cases that demand further explanation. Since ARM templates provide the source resources and configurations, and Azure becomes the platform for target resources and their configurations, there can be a mismatch between these two configurations. The mismatch could be resources missing in either of the locations or configuration drifts between resources.

How does Incremental take care of these differences?

The following are the different cases:

- **Resources in the template but not in the Azure platform**: Incremental deployment will create these resources on Azure and configure them according to the template-provided configuration.
- **Resources in the template and also in the Azure platform**: Incremental deployment will not touch these resources if the configuration matches. However, if there are configuration differences, the deployment will try to configure Azure resource with the template-provided configuration. If the configuration does not change the type, location, or any property that modifies the nature of the resource, the application of the template configuration is successful, otherwise it results in an error.
- **Resources in Azure but not in the template**: Incremental deployment will not touch these resources.

How to create and apply configuration in the case of Complete deployments

Let's see how Azure creates resources and applies configuration in the case of Complete deployments:

- **Resources in the template but not in the Azure platform**: Complete deployment will create these resources on Azure and configure them according to the template-provided configuration.
- **Resources in the template and also in the Azure platform**: Complete deployment will not touch these resources if the configuration matches. However, if there are configuration differences, the deployment will try to configure Azure resource with the template-provided configuration. If the configuration does not change the type, location, or any property that modifies the nature of the resource, the application of the template configuration is successful, otherwise it results in an error.

- **Resources in Azure but not in the template**: Complete deployment will delete these resources:

Existing resources in Azure	Resources in template	Incremental deployment	Complete deployment
Resource A (config X)	Resource A (config X)	Resource A (config X)	Resource A (config X)
Resource B (config X)	Resource B (config Y)	Resource B (config Y)	Resource B (config Y)
Resource C		Resource C	
	Resource D	Resource D	Resource D

Parameters

Parameters are well known **constructs** in programming languages. They are generally found within function declaration. They are placeholders filled up by values at runtime provided by the caller. Parameters in ARM templates are no different. Parameters are like fill-in-the-blanks, and these blanks are filled up with values by the caller.

Parameters help to make a template generic and customizable. Instead of hardcoding the values, data can be supplied at runtime and the template deployment can work with new set of incoming data. Parameters also make templates reusable across environments and subscriptions.

Note that there can be maximum of 255 parameters in an ARM template (there are ways to work around this limitation by using object data types for parameters) and using runtime values generated during deployment rather than defining parameters in ARM templates.

Structure of a parameter in an ARM template

Parameters are defined within the `parameters` section. The next example declares a parameter named `storageAccountName`. This parameter specifies the name of the Azure storage account.

Note that the `storageAccountName` parameter is of the `string` type.

The JSON is as follows:

```
"parameters": {
    "storageAccountName": {
      "type" : "string"
    }
}
```

There can be multiple `parameters` defined by commas within the same `parameters` section. `storageAccountName` and `storageAccountType` are defined parameters both of type `string`.

The JSON is as follows:

```
"parameters": {
    "storageAccountName": {
      "type" : "string"
    },

    "storageAccountType": {
      "type" : "string"
    }
}
```

A parameter structure is shown next. A parameter has a default value if the caller does not provide a value for it, it can also constrain the incoming value to a certain extent for integer values by applying minimum and maximum value. Similarly it can constrain the length of an array or string by applying minimum and maximum length. It also provides a provision to declare allowed values within a parameter which is similar to enumerations in any programming language. `allowedValues` is an array that contains the list of values allowed for the parameter. If the domain values are limited and already known, it is a good practice to set constraints using the `allowedValues` element.

The JSON is as follows:

```
"parameters": {
    "<parameter-name>" : {
        "type" : "<type-of-parameter-value>",
        "defaultValue": "<default-value-of-parameter>",
        "allowedValues": [ "<array-of-allowed-values>" ],
        "minValue": <minimum-value-for-int>,
        "maxValue": <maximum-value-for-int>,
        "minLength": <minimum-length-for-string-or-array>,
        "maxLength": <maximum-length-for-string-or-array-parameters>,
```

```
            "metadata": {
                "description": "<description-of-the-parameter>"
            }
        }
    }
}
```

An example of declaring an array type parameter is shown next. In this example, the default value comprises an array with three elements, each separated by comma.

The JSON is as follows:

```
"parameters": {
    "networkSubnetIPRanges": {
      "type": "array",
      "defaultValue": ["10.0.0.1/24", "10.0.1.0/24", "10.0.2.1/24"],
      "metadata": {
        "description": "Subnet IP address scheme for virtual network"
      }
    }
  }
```

Referencing a parameter within a template

Parameters can be referenced by using the `parameters` function provided by the ARM templates infrastructure. This function allows us to use the value stored in the parameter to configure any resource. `parameters` can be referenced from the `variables`, `resources`, and `outputs` sections of the same template.

In the following example, the SKU name property of the storage instance resource references the `storageAccountType` parameter value.

The JSON is as follows:

```
    {
        "type": "Microsoft.Storage/storageAccounts",
        "name": "[variables('storageAccountName')]",
       "apiVersion": "2018-02-01",
        "location": "[resourceGroup().location]",
        "sku": {
          "name": "[parameters('storageAccountType')]"
        },
        "kind": "Storage"
    }
```

Grouping parameters

An important recent update to ARM templates was the usage of the object data type to parameters. A parameter of the object type can accept any valid JSON from external resources as its input at runtime. This helps colocate parameters for a resource and helps form a natural grouping of properties. The same parameter can also define a default object if the external source does not provide a value for this parameter.

Grouping parameters is also a workaround to overcome the limitation of 255 parameters in a template.

Grouping using objects makes it easy for a caller to specify parameter values, which is much more intuitive and easier to comprehend the parameters. For example, we could group all storage-related parameters so that they aren't scattered throughout an ARM template.

Once object parameters are defined, they can be referenced from within any section of the template. A complete example using the `object` parameter to provision a storage account is shown next.

The ARM Template code is as follows:

```
{
 "$schema": "https://schema.management.azure.com/schemas/2015-01-01/deploymentTemplate.json#",
 "contentVersion": "1.0.0.0",
 "parameters": {
     "storageAccountConfiguration": {
         "type" : "object",
         "defaultValue" : {
             "name" : "sdw543fggsdfsd",
             "apiVersion" : "2018-02-01",
             "sku" : {
                 "name" : "Standard_LRS"
             }
         }
     }
 },
 "variables": {
 },
 "resources": [
 {
     "type": "Microsoft.Storage/storageAccounts",
     "name": "[parameters('storageAccountConfiguration').name]",
     "apiVersion":
```

```
    "[parameters('storageAccountConfiguration').apiVersion]",
      "location": "[resourceGroup().location]",
      "sku": {
          "name": "[parameters('storageAccountConfiguration').sku.name]",
      },
      "kind": "Storage"
      }
  ],
  "outputs": {
      "storageDetails": {
          "type": "string",
          "value": "[concat(parameters('storageAccountConfiguration').name,
  parameters('storageAccountConfiguration').sku.name)]"
          }
      }
  }
```

Variables

Variables are very similar to parameters in that they help to keep templates generic and maintainable. Modifying the value of a variable at a single place helps to update its value in all the places it is referenced from. However, there are a few notable differences between variables and parameters.

`variables` are defined and assigned values within the template itself, while values for `parameters` come from external sources. `variables` do not have data types declared explicitly, they do not have any facility to apply constraints or add description.

Possibly the best use case for `variables` is any data that is used multiple times within template should be replaced by variables. `variables` are name-value pairs where the value can be as simple as a literal string or a complex JSON object or array.

Variables are defined within the `variables` section of template. The next code listing shows different variable declaration types. The `storageType` variable is a simple variable with a literal string as its value. The `storageName` variable value is also a literal string; however, the string is generated using functions and expressions at runtime during time of deployment. The `api-version` variable has an array as its value with couple of elements in it, and the `virtualMachineOSType` variable is composed of complex JSON objects with multiple hierarchies within it.

The JSON is as follows:

```json
"variables": {
    "storageType": "Standard_LRS",
    "storageName": "[concat(parameters('storageAccountConfiguration'), resourceGroup().name)]",
    "api-version": ["2018-02-01", "2017-06-01"],
    "virtualMachineOSType": {
        "linux": {
            "imageReference": {
                "publisher": "Canonical",
                "offer": "UbuntuServer",
                "sku": "16.04.0-LTS",
                "version": "latest"
            }
        },
        "windows": {
            "imageReference": {
                "publisher": "MicrosoftWindowsServer",
                "offer": "WindowsServer",
                "sku": "2016-Datacenter",
                "version": "latest"
            }
        }
    }
}
```

Accessing variables

Variables can be accessed within other `variables`, `resources`, and `outputs` in the ARM template. Variables are accessed using the `variables` function passing the identifier for the variable.

The next code listing shows the usage of `variables` in the resources section. Note that arrays are accessed using their index position is square brackets.

The JSON is as follows:

```json
"resources": [
    {
        "type": "Microsoft.Storage/storageAccounts",
        "name": "[variables('storageName')]",
        "apiVersion": "[variables('api-version')[0]]",
        "location": "[resourceGroup().location]",
        "sku": {
            "name": "[variables('storageType')]"
```

```
        },
        "kind": "Storage"
    }
]
```

We will revisit `variables` in `Chapter 4`, *Advance Template Features*, to show the usage of the `copy` function along with the `variables`.

Summary

Congratulations! You have created your first ARM template and deployed it into Azure. This chapter covered quite a lot of ground. We started by creating a development environment and ways to author ARM templates using Visual Studio and Visual Studio Code. We discussed the structure of ARM templates and their main constituents. From there, we looked at ways to deploy ARM templates using Azure PowerShell, CLI, and portal. We also explored the subject of `parameters` in detail. We covered the parameter structure, declaring `parameters`, and using `parameters` in ARM templates. We also covered `variables` in depth, along with some best practices.

In the next chapter, we will look at output, functions, and expressions, and use some of the concepts we explored in this chapter.

3
Understanding Core Elements of ARM Templates

Now that we know the basic outline and structure of an ARM template, and we also know how to declare and use `variables` and `parameters`, it's time to move to other important aspects of ARM templates. In this chapter, we will look into some of the most important concepts related to ARM templates. ARM templates provide a foundation for the way environments and resources are provisioned on Azure, while the `resources` object is the place where all resources are declared, defined, and configured. In this chapter, we will look at the `resources` object, along with the `outputs` object, which is the way to return or generate `outputs` from ARM templates. Outputs play a significant role in providing feedback to the ARM template deployed regarding the state of execution, and other runtime values that can be of importance for testing and usage in other dependent ARM templates.

As we discuss resource and output JSON objects, you will discover that additional capabilities are needed to configure the objects using runtime values and objects. Without the ability to compute, configure, or generate runtime values based on a given context, it is difficult to write generic, modular, reusable, and maintainable templates. Azure ARM templates provide expressions that write constructs to be evaluated at runtime while deploying the template to generate values. These expressions can use Azure ARM templates' numerous functions to ease the task of determining and generating appropriate values.

In this chapter, we will use many functions and write numerous expressions to explain their usage. Specifically, we will cover the following topics:

- ARM template expressions
- ARM template functions
- The `resources` object
- A complete template
- Nesting resources
- Understanding `dependsOn`
- Using references
- Understanding `resourceId`
- Using linked templates
- Using nested templates

ARM template expressions

Expressions can, at times, be confusing to understand. Expressions often look very similar to program statements, so it can be difficult to distinguish a statement from an expression, and so on. Expressions are written to be evaluated at runtime before returning a value; the value can only be ascertained at runtime. Statements, however, are program code that are executed to perform an action, such as assignments and looping. An expression is comprised of variables, operators, literals, and functions that work together to generate runtime values.

Generally, we declare variables using a specific data type and then use that variable at multiple points within the program. Expressions are similar to variables; however, the variable itself is instead constructed and evaluated at runtime.

Let's understand expressions with the help of an example, as follows:

```
"count": "[length(parameters('resourceGroupInfo'))]"
```

In the preceding example, the value of the `count` key is dependent on an expression. Here, the expression is using a couple of functions, that is, `length` and `parameters`, which are used to find the length of data stored in the `resourceGroupInfo` parameter. The expression is evaluated at runtime while deploying the template to Azure, and the generated value is then assigned to the `count` key.

Expressions in ARM templates are written within square brackets, `[`, at the start of an expression, and `]` at the end of an expression. The entire expression should be within double-quotes, `""`.

The return value from an expression can be any of the following:

- ARM template-supported data types, including string, Boolean, and integers
- A JSON object
- A JSON array

ARM template functions

Functions are units of code execution that are made up of multiple statements. Functions help to improve the reusability of code by encapsulating statements into reusable nuggets that can be invoked or called from multiple places. Azure ARM templates provide multiple functions to make the authoring of advanced templates both easy and versatile.

The output of an ARM template is always deterministic, meaning that no matter the number of times a template is executed or deployed, the end output will always be the same. It is for this reason that functions available with the ARM template do not provide functions based on randomness, date and time, or any other non-deterministic variable.

Almost all programming languages have functions as one of their important constructs. Functions are categorized to accept parameters from a caller and then return output after executing a set of code statements; ARM template functions are very similar to programming language functions. ARM templates provide multiple out-of-the-box functions for use within expressions. Examples of these functions include mathematical functions, such as add (for adding two integers), sub (for subtracting two integers), and mul, which is used for multiplying two integers.

It is important to note that functions can only be used within expressions in ARM templates, as we have already seen in a number of our examples.

Functions can be nested within other functions to create and solve complex problems. For example, if you want to generate a unique storage account name that has no uppercase letters and is based on user-provided input, this can be written using multiple functions in one expression, as follows:

```
"storageName": "[concat(toLower(parameters('storageNamePrefix')),
uniqueString(resourceGroup().id))]"
```

Here, the `concat` function concatenates multiple values together. The `toLower` function converts its input text into lowercase, the `parameters` function accesses user-provided input, `uniqueString` generates a hash of its input, and finally, the `resourceGroup` function provides details of a current resource group.

Resources

Resources are the crux of writing ARM templates; without them, there is no point in writing a template. As we saw in the first two chapters, resources in Azure can be created in a number of different ways, including using portal, PowerShell scripts, REST APIs, and much more. However, the most important, and also DevOps-friendly, way to create an environment using a declarative language is through ARM templates. ARM templates make the entire process of creating and managing resources predictable and consistent.

Resources are quite unique, even within ARM templates. They have their own set of mandatory and optional properties. There are varying types of resources, and each one differs in how it's configured and whether it has nested resources.

Resource names

Every resource should have a unique `name` within a resource group. It is with this `name` that they are identified in Azure and the `reference` function also uses it to access the resource. The `name` is the identifier for a resource; therefore, every resource has a `name` element in an ARM template. Note that it is mandatory to provide a unique value to an element in the resource group, as follows:

```
"name": "ST-R001-EASTUS-PROD"
```

`name` should be assigned a string value, but it can also be composed of a literal character or assigned a value using an expression. The following example illustrates how to assign an expression to the `name` element in a template. The value from the expression is generated during deployment and then assigned to the `name` element as follows:

```
"name": "[toUpper(parameter('UserInputforName'))]"
```

Resource types

Every resource should also have a `type`. The `type` determines which resource should be provisioned during deployment. This is also a mandatory property, without which Azure has no way of knowing which resource it should create. Examples of resources include virtual machines, storage accounts, public IP addresses, and many more. Each resource is referred by its `type`, and they are contained within another component known as a **resource provider**. To refer to a resource, both the resource provider and its `type` should be mentioned within the ARM template. Think of it as declaring a variable in a programming language and specifying the type for it. In other words, every resource should have a `type` element in the ARM template, and it is mandatory to provide a value that is valid and available.

The following example shows a resource type, `sites`, that is part of `Microsoft.Web` resource provider and assigned to the `type` element:

```
"type": "Microsoft.Web/sites"
```

Another example of the `type` element is as follows:

```
"type": "Microsoft.Storage/storageAccounts"
```

API Version

We know that resources have a type, and that they are continuously getting updated by Azure team either for fixing bugs or implementing new features. The new version might have breaking changes. For example, if you have written a template consisting of resources without providing a specific version number and execute the same template sometime in future, you may get unexpected results in such cases because without a specific version, latest version is used. To ensure that such problems do not arise, the Azure team assigns a version number to each resource and updates it whenever a breaking change is made. The version number is usually a date and is known as the **API version** in ARM templates. You must assign a value to a resource's API version. It is also important to understand that an API version often has different values for each resource; this is because each resource has its own independent life cycle development process.

The following example illustrates using `apiVersion` in a storage account:

```
"apiVersion": "2018-02-01"
```

Other API versions for the preceding storage account include the following:

```
2018-03-01-preview
2018-02-01
2017-10-01
2017-06-01
2016-12-01
2016-05-01
2016-01-01
2015-06-15
2015-05-01-preview
```

In fact, Azure PowerShell has a cmdlet, `Get-AzureRmResourceProvider`, which provides all existing API versions and locations of a resource.

Executing the following code provides the API versions of a resource supported by an Azure storage account:

```
(Get-AzureRmResourceProvider -ProviderNamespace
Microsoft.Storage).ResourceTypes[0].ApiVersions
```

The API versions available for a public IP address resource are as follows:

```
2018-07-01
2018-06-01
2018-05-01
2018-04-01
2018-03-01
2018-02-01
2018-01-01
2017-11-01
2017-10-01
2017-09-01
2017-08-01
2017-06-01
2017-04-01
2017-03-01
2016-12-01
2016-11-01
2016-10-01
2016-09-01
2016-08-01
2016-07-01
2016-06-01
```

```
2016-03-30
2015-06-15
2015-05-01-preview
2014-12-01-preview
```

Astute readers might have noticed a number of API version values that include `preview`. This is because they are under development, and may change or be cleaned up at a later date. Note that it is not recommended to rely on a preview version of a resource.

As well as providing a specific resource version, it is also possible to assign the latest API version. This will ensure that users enable the most recent API version whenever a template is used in deployment. Once again, it is not recommended to use the latest API version, simply because the resource may have evolved significantly over time.

The find the latest API version, use the following code: `"apiVersion"`: `"latest"`.

Resource properties

Each resource should be configured appropriately for its purpose. Configuration data is provided to all resources using properties in ARM templates. Again, it is important to understand that each resource will have separate configuration requirements, and a different set of properties may be required. We advise readers to go through the properties of each resource before using them in ARM templates. These properties can be read at https://docs.microsoft.com/en-us/azure/templates/.

The properties of a `serverfarms` resource is shown in the next code listing. Here, there are resource-specific property elements, such as the `sku` which is unique to the resource:

```
{
    "type": "Microsoft.Web/serverfarms",
    "kind": "app",
    "name": "[parameters('appServicePlanName')]",
    "location": "[resourceGroup().location]",
    "apiVersion": "2016-09-01",
    "properties": {
      "name": "[parameters('appServicePlanName')]"
    },
    "sku": {
    "Tier": "[parameters('appServicePlanSkuTier')]",
      "Name": "[parameters('appServicePlanSkuName')]"
    }
}
```

Resource locations

Azure provides multiple regions as standard. Resources can be deployed to any of the available regions. These regions are known as **locations** in ARM templates. It is important to understand that not all resources are available in all Azure locations. For example, Azure may initially introduce a resource to one location before rolling it out elsewhere.

In the following example, we see locations at work. Here, the storage account will be deployed in the `East US` location, as follows:

```
"location": "East US"
```

Using the same `Get-AzureRmResourceProvider` cmdlet, it is possible to get all supported locations for a resource. The Azure Storage account is currently available at the following locations:

```
PS C:\Users\rites> (Get-AzureRmResourceProvider -ProviderNamespace
Microsoft.Network).ResourceTypes[1].Locations
West US
East US
North Europe
West Europe
East Asia
Southeast Asia
North Central US
South Central US
Central US
East US 2
Japan East
Japan West
Brazil South
Australia East
Australia Southeast
Central India
South India
West India
Canada Central
Canada East
West Central US
West US 2
UK West
UK South
Korea Central
Korea South
France Central
```

There is also a function called `resourceGroup()`, which returns the `location` property of a current resource group. If the resource is deployed at the same location as that of the resource group, then this property can be used as follows:

```
"location": "[resourceGroup().location]"
```

Resources and nested resources

There are resources that have a parent-child dependency on other resources. The existence of a child resource is dependent on the parent resource; if the parent resource is not available, the child resource cannot be provisioned. Although each resource can be declared and defined as top-level resource in an ARM template, the child resources can also be defined as nested resources within parent resource. There can be multiple levels of such nesting in an ARM template.

Let's understand this concept with the help of an example. Azure SQL needs two major resources to host databases. They are

- Azure logical SQL Server
- Azure database

The logical server acts as a parent to the Azure database resource, and the Azure database resource cannot be provisioned unless the logical server is already available. We will take a more in-depth look at nested resources later after a few sections in this chapter.

Outputs

Outputs are optional segments within an ARM template. Although they are optional, they play a very important role in the resource runtime values to the caller. This is very similar to how a function returns a value in a programming language. Of course, the function may choose not to return anything, but it is always considered good practice to return the execution status. ARM templates can be treated like functions where the caller provides parameters, executes the ARM template and the ARM template returns `outputs` as return value.

Understanding Core Elements of ARM Templates

Defining `outputs` in an ARM template means listing all outputs along with their types. An example of an output is shown as follows. In this example, the output is a JSON object comprising all details related to a storage account:

```
"outputs": {
    "storage": {
      "type": "object",
      "value": "[reference(parameters('storageAccountName'))]"
    }
}
```

In the preceding example, the `outputs` segment consists of a single output, `storage`. Each output is a JSON object and consists of two properties, `type` and `value`. `Type` refers to the data type of a returned output, and can be of any type supported by ARM templates (such as integer, Boolean, string, array, SecureString, object, or SecureObject). `Value` refers to the actual value associated with an output. The value can be determined statically by hardcoding it, or it can be generated at runtime using expressions. It is considered a good practice to determine output dynamically at runtime using expressions.

A complete template

We have now covered all of the essential elements needed when creating a template. The following code shows a template including `parameters`, `variables`, `resources`, and `outputs`. This code is available in the `chapter-3 - listing1.txt` file in the accompanying chapter code:

```
{
  "$schema": "https://schema.management.azure.com/schemas/2015-01-01/deploymentTemplate.json#",
  "contentVersion": "1.0.0.0",
  "parameters": {
    "customTags": {
      "type": "object",
      "defaultValue": {
        "Dept": "Technology",
        "Environment": "Production"
      }
    },
    "storageAccountName": { "type": "string" },
    "storageAccountType": {"type": "string"}
  },
  "variables": {
  },
```

```
    "resources": [
      {
        "apiVersion": "2018-02-01",
        "name": "[parameters('storageAccountName')]",
        "location": "[resourceGroup().location]",
        "type": "Microsoft.Storage/storageAccounts",
        "tags": "[parameters('customTags')]",
        "sku": {
          "name": "[parameters('storageAccountType')]"
        },
        "kind": "Storage",
        "properties": {
          "encryption": {
            "services": {
              "blob": {
                "enabled": true
              },
              "file": null
            },
            "keySource": "Microsoft.Storage"
          }
        }
      }
    ],
    "outputs": {
      "storage": {
        "type": "object",
        "value": "[reference(parameters('storageAccountName'))]"
      }
    }
}
```

Nesting resources

We have already learned that resources can have parent resources, and that child resources can be provisioned only after a parent resource is already provisioned. In the next example, we will provision a parent resource (`sites`) using ARM template. You will notice that the `sites` resource has an internal resources element. This element can declare multiple child resources within it. A resource of `connectionstrings` type is created within this resources section. This particular resource acts like a child resource for the sites parent resource. If you think about it, a `connectionstrings` resource can only be contained within a web app (sites); it does not make sense to deploy a `connectionstrings` resource without a web app, because `connectionstrings` are eventually placed within the `web.config` file of a web app.

Understanding Core Elements of ARM Templates

The complete code for the following template is available in the `chapter-3 - listing2.txt` file in the accompanying chapter code.

The following template defines a number of `parameters` that will configure the App Services Plan. Notice how default values, minimum values, and metadata elements are used to augment the behavior of the `skuCapacity` parameter, as follows:

```
"parameters": {
    "skuName": {
        "type": "string",
        "defaultValue": "F1"
    },
    "skuCapacity": {
        "type": "int",
        "defaultValue": 1,
        "minValue": 1,
        "metadata": {
            "description": "Describes plan's instance count"
        }
    }
}
```

There are a couple of variables declared in the `variables` section, as shown in the next code listing. These variables relate to the name of the App Service Plan and Web App resource.

```
"variables": {
    "hostingPlanName": "[concat('hostingplan', uniqueString(resourceGroup().id))]",
    "webSiteName": "[concat('webSite', uniqueString(resourceGroup().id))]"
}
```

This template contains two top-level `resources` - `Microsoft.Web/serverfarms` and `Microsoft.Web/sites`. The `Microsoft.Web/sites` resource contains an inner resource of type `config`.

The code shown next relates to resource of type `Microsoft.Web/serverfarms`:

```
{
    "apiVersion": "2016-03-01",
    "name": "[variables('hostingPlanName')]",
    "type": "Microsoft.Web/serverfarms",
    "location": "[parameters('location')]",
    "tags": {
        "displayName": "HostingPlan"
    },
    "sku": {
```

```
            "name": "[parameters('skuName')]",
            "capacity": "[parameters('skuCapacity')]"
        },
        "properties": {
            "name": "[variables('hostingPlanName')]"
        }
    }
```

The code related to `Microsoft.Web/sites` resource is shown in the next code listing.

As mentioned before, this resource contains an inner-resource. The inner-resource is dependent on its parent resource and should not be provisioned before provisioning the parent resource. The `dependsOn` element in the inner-resource ensures that the inner resource starts provisioning only after the parent resource has been provisioned. The inner-resource has access to the `parameters` and `variables` defined within the template.

```
    {
        "apiVersion": "2016-03-01",
        "name": "[variables('webSiteName')]",
        "type": "Microsoft.Web/sites",
        "location": "[parameters('location')]",
        "dependsOn": [
            "[variables('hostingPlanName')]"
        ],
        "properties": {
            "name": "[variables('webSiteName')]",
            "severFarmId": "[resourceId('Microsoft.Web/serverfarms', variables('hostingPlanName'))]"
        },
        "resources": [
            {
                "apiVersion": "2016-03-01",
                "type": "config",
                "name": "connectionstrings",
                "dependsOn": [
                    "[variables('webSiteName')]"
                ],
                "properties": {
                    "DefaultConnection": {
                        "value": "[concat('Data Source=tcp:', reference(concat('Microsoft.Sql/servers/', variables('sqlserverName'))).fullyQualifiedDomainName, ',1433;Initial Catalog=', variables('databaseName'), ';User Id=', parameters('sqlAdministratorLogin'), '@', reference(concat('Microsoft.Sql/servers/', variables('sqlserverName'))).fullyQualifiedDomainName, ';Password=', parameters('sqlAdministratorLoginPassword'), ';')]",
```

```
                    "type": "SQLAzure"
                }
            }
        ]
    }
```

The final segment of this template contains an `outputs` element that returns back data, as shown in the next code snippet.

```
"outputs": {
    "siteUri": {
        "type": "string",
        "value": "[reference(concat('Microsoft.Web/sites/',
variables('webSiteName'))).hostnames[0]]"
    }
}
```

Understanding dependsOn

There are often multiple resources in an ARM template, and, by default, they are all provisioned in parallel. However, this default behavior can be modified using the `dependsOn` element. `dependsOn` helps to define dependencies between resources within an ARM template. If there are resources that are dependent on another resource availability, the resources should be provisioned only after those independent resources have been provisioned. `dependsOn` does not create a parent-child relationship between resources, however; it just mandates the deployment sequence of resources. Each resource can declare multiple resources within its `dependsOn` section, but they will only be provisioned after all declared resources are provisioned. It is important to note that there can be multiple levels of dependencies between Azure resources.

The `dependsOn` element accepts a JSON array as its input, as shown in the following example:

```
"dependsOn": [
  "[parameters('storageAccountName')]"
]
```

In this example, there is just one resource identifier supplied to `dependsOn`: the storage account name. This means that the current resource will be provisioned only after the storage account is provisioned. Let's see a complete example of `dependsOn`.

In the following example, two resources are provisioned, `serverfarm` and `sites`. These are also known as **hosting plan** and **web app** in Azure. Every web app needs a hosting plan a.k.a `serverfarm`. It is important that `serverfarm` resource is created before the web app resource. Although these are the two resources in the template and they can be provisioned in parallel, it is quite possible that sites resource tries to get provisioned before the `serverfarm` resource. This can lead to errors and unexpected results. In short, executing a template containing inter-dependent resources without defining the dependencies might lead to unpredictable results.

The `Microsoft.Web/serverfarms` resource does not have any `dependsOn` element. However, the `Microsoft.Web/sites` resource does have dependsOn element and it refers to the `Microsoft.Web/serverfarms` resource by its name. Defining the `Microsoft.Web/serverfarms` resource name as a variable is useful as it can be repeatedly used at multiple locations. When this template is deployed, first `Microsoft.Web/serverfarms` resource is provisioned followed by the `Microsoft.Web/sites` resource.

The following template is available in the file `chapter-3 - listing3.txt` with the accompanying chapter code.

The ARM template accepts a couple of `parameters` related to the App Service Plan and Web App resource as shown next:

```
"parameters": {
    "skuName": {
        "type": "string",
        "defaultValue": "F1"
    },
    "skuCapacity": {
        "type": "int",
        "defaultValue": 1,
        "minValue": 1
    }
}
```

In the next code snippet, there are a couple of `variables` declared in the `variables` section. They relate to the names of App Service Plan and Web App resource:

```
"variables": {
    "hostingPlanName": "[concat('hostingplan', uniqueString(resourceGroup().id))]",
    "webSiteName": "[concat('webSite', uniqueString(resourceGroup().id))]"
}
```

Understanding Core Elements of ARM Templates

The `resources` section contains two top-level `resources` of type `Microsoft.Web/serverfarms` and `Microsoft.Web/sites`. The code relating to `Microsoft.Web/serverfarms` is shown next:

```
{
    "apiVersion": "2016-03-01",
    "name": "[variables('hostingPlanName')]",
    "type": "Microsoft.Web/serverfarms",
    "location": "[parameters('location')]",
    "tags": {
        "displayName": "HostingPlan"
    },
    "sku": {
        "name": "[parameters('skuName')]",
        "capacity": "[parameters('skuCapacity')]"
    },
    "properties": {
        "name": "[variables('hostingPlanName')]"
    }
}
```

The code related to `Microsoft.Web/sites` is shown in the following snippet. Notice how this resource declares its dependency on the previous resource, `Microsoft.Web/serverfarms`. Remember, this resource will only be provisioned after its parent resource has been:

```
{
 "apiVersion": "2016-03-01",
 "name": "[variables('webSiteName')]",
 "type": "Microsoft.Web/sites",
 "location": "[resourceGroup().location]",
 "dependsOn": [
     "[variables('hostingPlanName')]"
   ],
 "properties": {
     "name": "[variables('webSiteName')]",
         "serverFarmId": "[resourceId('Microsoft.Web/serverfarms',
variables('hostingPlanName'))]"
     }
 }
```

The last segment of this template contains an `outputs` element that returns back data as shown in the following snippet:

```
"outputs": {
    "siteUri": {
        "type": "string",
```

[66]

```
            "value": "[reference(concat('Microsoft.Web/sites/',
variables('webSiteName'))).hostnames[0]]"
        }
}
```

By using `dependsOn`, it is possible to create a complete graph of resources based on their dependencies.

Using references

The `reference` function is an advanced concept in ARM templates and one of the most important and useful functions. Before going into the `reference` function any further, let's get a bit deeper into the deployment process of ARM templates.

When an ARM template is submitted to Azure, the entire ARM template is read, parsed, and validated. During parsing, all expressions and functions are evaluated to generate the real values behind them and then use them to configure the resources. There are times when we need a value from a resource to configure another resource. For example, the SQL Server firewall rules require IP addresses of all virtual machines for whitelisting. During ARM template deployment, both virtual machines and Azure SQL resources will be provisioned, and as we know, `dependsOn` can be used between them to ensure that virtual machines are provisioned before Azure SQL. To supply these dynamic virtual machine IP addresses to Azure SQL Server during deployment, `reference` function can be used.

The `reference` function, as the name suggests, refers to another resource or its properties. Since references are evaluated at runtime, it is not possible to use this function in the parameters and variables section. `Reference` functions can be used within the `outputs` and `resources` sections only. `Reference` cannot be used within a nested template.

The syntax for the `reference` function is as follows:

```
"[reference(name of resource or resource identifier)]"
```

Understanding Core Elements of ARM Templates

In the following example, the reference is made to the SQL Server resource using its own name, which is provided during deployment by the user:

```
"[reference(parameters('sqlServerName'))]"
```

The `reference` function takes the following three parameters:

- **Name or identifier of the resource**: This is a mandatory parameter and must be supplied
- **API version of the resource**: This is an optional parameter and should be provided only if the resource referred to by the `reference` function is not provisioned within the template
- **Full**: This parameter determines whether the entire generated output of a resource should be referenced

The return value of the `reference` function is dynamic; it can be any data type supported by ARM templates, such as a JSON array, JSON object, string, integers, or a Boolean. The author of an ARM template should understand the return types available and assign an appropriate element within the template.

For example, the return value from the `[reference(parameters('sqlServerName'))]` execution has the following output:

```
"SQLServer": {
  "type": "object",
  "value": "[reference(parameters('sqlServerName'))]"
},
```

As you can see, it is a JSON object that contains all runtime output that has been generated by Azure while deploying the resource, as shown in the following screenshot:

```
Outputs       :
              Name              Type                            Value
              ==============    ==========================      ==========
              sqlServer         Object                          {
                "administratorLogin": "citynextadmin",
                "version": "12.0",
                "state": "Ready",
                "fullyQualifiedDomainName": "riteshsrvunq01.database.windows.net"
              }
```

It is also possible to extract a single property from the referenced generated output:

```
"SQLServer": {
        "type": "object",
        "value":
"[reference(parameters('sqlServerName')).fullyQualifiedDomainName]"
    },
```

[68]

The output of the preceding `reference` function is shown in the next screenshot:

```
Outputs        :
                Name               Type                    Value
                =============      =================       =========
                sqlServer          String                  riteshsrvunq01.database.windows.net
```

The next example shows the usage of all three `parameters`. The database resource is not deployed using the same template, so the second parameter becomes mandatory and the third one generates complete details of the resource:

```
"[reference(resourceid('Microsoft.SQL/servers/databases',
parameters('sqlServerName'), parameters('sqlDatabaseName')),'2017-10-01-
preview', 'full')]"
```

The result of using `reference` function in an output section is shown in the next screenshot:

```
Name                Type            Value
============        ==========      =========
sqlServer           Object          {
                                      "administratorLogin": "citynextadmin",
                                      "version": "12.0",
                                      "state": "Ready",
                                      "fullyQualifiedDomainName": "riteshsrvunq01.database.windows.net"
                                    }
sqlDatabase         Object          {
                                      "apiVersion": "2017-10-01-preview",
                                      "location": "westeurope",
                                      "sku": {
                                        "name": "Standard",
                                        "tier": "Standard",
                                        "capacity": 10
                                      },
                                      "kind": "v12.0,user",
                                      "properties": {
                                        "collation": "SQL_Latin1_General_CP1_CI_AS",
                                        "maxSizeBytes": 107374182400,
                                        "status": "Online",
                                        "databaseId": "3332c4ab-f58f-433a-8ea6-e8d38ef856c4",
                                        "creationDate": "2018-08-20T07:30:17.173Z",
                                        "currentServiceObjectiveName": "S0",
                                        "requestedServiceObjectiveName": "S0",
                                        "defaultSecondaryLocation": "northeurope",
                                        "catalogCollation": "SQL_Latin1_General_CP1_CI_AS",
                                        "zoneRedundant": false,
                                        "earliestRestoreDate": "2018-08-20T07:30:51.453Z",
                                        "readScale": "Disabled",
                                        "currentSku": {
                                          "name": "Standard",
                                          "tier": "Standard",
                                          "capacity": 10
                                        }
                                      },
                                      "subscriptionId": "9755ffce-e94b-4332-9be8-1ade15e78909",
                                      "resourceGroupName": "CLIDeployment",
                                      "resourceId": "Microsoft.SQL/servers/riteshsrvunq01/databases/riteshdbunq01",
                                      "referenceApiVersion": "2017-10-01-preview",
                                      "condition": true,
                                      "isConditionTrue": true,
                                      "isTemplateResource": false,
                                      "isAction": false,
                                      "provisioningOperation": "Read"
                                    }
```

The ARM template code shown in the following example is available in the `chapter-3 - listing4.txt` file from the accompanying chapter code.

The next template shows the usage of the `references` function. The template code has `parameters`, `resources`, and `outputs` sections.

The `parameters`, section is shown next and it declares parameters related to Azure SQL Server and database configuration:

```
    "parameters": {
        "sqlServerName": {
            "type": "string"
        },
        "sqlServerAdministratorLoginName": {
            "type": "string"
        },
        "sqlServerAdministratorLoginPassword": {
            "type": "securestring"
        },
        "sqlDatabaseCollation": {
            "type": "string",
            "defaultValue": "SQL_Latin1_General_CP1_CI_AS"
        },
        "sqlDatabaseEdition": {
            "type": "string",
            "defaultValue": "Standard"
        },
        "sqlDatabaseMaxSizeBytes": {
            "type": "string",
            "defaultValue": "107374182400"
        },
        "sqlDatabaseName": {
            "type": "string"
        },
        "sqlDatabaseRequestedServiceObjectiveName": {
            "type": "string",
            "defaultValue": "S2"
        }
    }
```

The `resources` section contains one parent resource with an inner resource. The parent resource creates a resource of `Microsoft.Sql/servers` type and an inner resource of the `Microsoft.Sql/servers/databases` type. The `Microsoft.Sql/servers` type represents an Azure SQL Server, and `Microsoft.Sql/servers/databases` represent a database within a server. Notice that the type value comprises of three elements. The first one is the name of the provider, the second is the parent resource type, and the third is the child resource type. The code for `resources` is shown next:

```
{
  "type": "Microsoft.Sql/servers",
  "kind": "v12.0",
  "name": "[parameters('sqlServerName')]",
  "location": "[resourceGroup().location]",
  "apiVersion": "2015-05-01-preview",
  "properties": {
      "administratorLogin":
"[parameters('sqlServerAdministratorLoginName')]",
      "administratorLoginPassword":
"[parameters('sqlServerAdministratorLoginPassword')]",
      "version": "12.0"
      },
  "resources": [
          {
          "type": "Microsoft.Sql/servers/databases",
          "name":
"[concat(parameters('sqlServerName'),'/',parameters('sqlDatabaseName'))]",
          "location": "[resourceGroup().location]",
          "apiVersion": "2017-10-01-preview",
          "dependsOn": [
              "[parameters('sqlServerName')]"
            ],
          "properties": {
              "edition": "[parameters('sqlDatabaseEdition')]",
              "collation": "[parameters('sqlDatabaseCollation')]",
              "maxSizeBytes": "[parameters('sqlDatabaseMaxSizeBytes')]",
              "requestedServiceObjectiveName": "
[parameters('sqlDatabaseRequestedServiceObjectiveName')]"
              }
          }
      ]
  }
```

The most interesting part of the preceding example is the `outputs` section, which declares three outputs: `SQLServerFQDN`, `SQLServer`, and `SQLDatabase`. The `FQDN` parameter is of the `string` type and the remaining two are of type objects. Notice how the values for all of these `outputs` are filled with runtime information using the `reference` function.

The last output is different compared to the previous two outputs. Again, notice that the `reference` function for the last output uses multiple arguments. The first parameter is the resource identifier and it uses the `resourceId` function to generate the identifier. The second parameter is the API version of the referenced resource and the third parameter is a switch that determines whether complete information should be generated. The `resourceId` function, shown in the next example, is explained in detail in the next section of this chapter:

```
"outputs": {
    "SQLServerFQDN": {
      "type": "string",
      "value":
"[reference(parameters('sqlServerName')).fullyQualifiedDomainName]"
    },
    "SQLServer": {
      "type": "object",
      "value": "[reference(parameters('sqlServerName'))]"
    },
    "SQLDatabase": {
      "type": "object",
      "value": "[reference(resourceid('Microsoft.SQL/servers/databases',
parameters('sqlServerName'), parameters('sqlDatabaseName')),'2017-10-01-
preview', 'full')]"
    }
  }
```

Understanding resourceId

Another important function used within an ARM template is the `resourceId` function. Every resource deployed on Azure has a friendly display name and can be used for referencing from both PowerShell and ARM templates. However, this display name is not used by Azure to identify resources.

Instead, Azure generates a unique URI for each deployed resource, which can be retrieved using the `resourceId`function. Resources can be a parent resource, child resource, or even a child resource of another child resource. They all have unique identifier and can be uniformly identified using the resourceId function.

The format generated by `resourceId` is shown in the next code snippet. The items in `{}` brackets are values that are replaced with actual values of resources and its context. Readers will notice that `resourceId` uses a pattern to generate its unique identifier. The first part is `subscriptions`, which is then followed by a unique subscription name. The second part is `resourceGroups`, also followed by a unique resource group name. The third part is the resource provider namespace, followed by the name of the resource type, and finally the name of the resource as shown next:

```
/subscriptions/{subscriptionId}/resourceGroups/{resourceGroupName}/providers/{resourceProviderNamespace}/{resourceType}/{resourceName}
```

The `resourceId` function takes five parameters. Two parameters are mandatory and the remaining three are optional. These optional parameters should be used in different situations as discussed next.

The syntax for the `resourceId` function is as follows:

```
resourceId([subscriptionId], [resourceGroupName], resourceType, resourceName1, [resourceName2]...)
```

`subscriptionId` is an optional parameter and should be used only when referring to a resource that is not available within a current subscription. Note that `subscriptionId` refers to a specific ID, not just a name.

`resourceGroupName` is an optional parameter and should be used only when referring to a resource that is not available within a current resource group.

The `resourceType` is a mandatory parameter and must be provided. Examples of `resourceType` that we have seen before include `Microsoft.Web/sites`, `Microsoft.storages/StorageAccounts`, and more.

`resourceName1` is also a mandatory parameter and should always be provided. This parameter refers to the value or name of a resource.

`resourceName2` should be used for child `resources`. For example, if you want to generate the `resourceId` of a database that is a child of the `resourcetype` server, the `resourceName2` parameter should be used with the appropriate database name.

Understanding Core Elements of ARM Templates

The return type of `resourceId` is always a string.

Let's now try to understand the applications of `resourceid` with the help of some examples.

In the following example, just two parameters are used. This is because the SQL server has been deployed using the same template:

```
"SQLServerResourceID": {
   "type": "string",
   "value": "[resourceid('Microsoft.SQL/servers',
parameters('sqlServerName'))]"
   },
```

The output for this execution is shown next.

```
/subscriptions/9755ffce-
e94b-4332-9be8-1ade15e78909/resourceGroups/CLIDeployment/providers/Microsof
t.SQL/servers/riteshsrvunq01
```

In the next example, a resource with a child resource is used for generating the `resourceid`:

```
"SQLDatabaseResourceID": {
   "type": "string",
   "value": "[resourceid('Microsoft.SQL/servers/databases',
parameters('sqlServerName'), parameters('sqlDatabaseName'))]"
   }
```

The output of previous expression is shown next:

```
/subscriptions/xxxxxxxx-xxxx-xxxx-xxxx-
xxxxxxxxxxxx/resourceGroups/CLIDeployment/providers/Microsoft.SQL/servers/r
iteshsrvunq01/databases/riteshdbunq01
```

The next example illustrates the usage of all five parameters:

```
"SQLDatabaseResourceIDfromDiffernetSubscription": {
    "type": "string",
    "value":
"[resourceid(subscription().subscriptionId,resourcegroup().name,'Microsoft.
SQL/servers/databases', parameters('sqlServerName'),
parameters('sqlDatabaseName'))]"
    }
```

[74]

The following output is very similar to that in the preceding example. Note that resources can be referred from different `subscription` and `resourceGroup` sections in an ARM template using this technique:

```
/subscriptions/9755ffce-e94b-4332-9be8-1ade15e78909/resourceGroups/CLIDeployment/providers/Microsoft.SQL/servers/riteshsrvunq01/databases/riteshdbunq01
```

Using linked templates

You should now have a greater understanding of how resources should be defined and configured in an ARM template. It is possible to write one large template that consists of hundreds of resources. The challenges of using a single template to define all resources are

- **Difficulty in changing templates**: With all resources in one template, any change will require a retest of the entire template, which can be a daunting and time-consuming task.
- **Difficulty in managing and maintaining templates**: Understanding a single template comprising of many resources is not easy. An increase in complexity can leave templates more vulnerable to error.

Modular templates can offer a solution to such challenges. Instead of having a single large template, it is possible to break down the templates into multiple, smaller templates, where each template has its own function and resource definition. This approach adopts the principle of single responsibility. This approach does not mean that there should be one template for each resource provisioned, however. Instead, it means that resources should be logically and physically grouped together based on their dependencies, life cycle, and region, and then implemented within a single template.

The beauty of writing modular templates is that it produces templates that are easy to read, understand, and maintain. It is also easier to make changes. Adding and removing individual templates can also be done without implicating the overall solution and any other resources.

Linked templates are multiple templates that are instructed by a master template to deploy resources. Nested templates can be implemented and invoked in ARM templates using the deployment resource. While configuring the deployment resource, it should be passed to the location of the nested template, which should be a well-defined location in reach of the deployment locations of the master template. The well-defined location could be an Azure storage account, VSTS release servers, or any other unique URI on the internet or intranet reachable from the master template. It cannot be on a local machine.

The following diagram explains nested deployments. As you can see, the **Master Template** is comprised of deployment resources that each invoke **Nested Templates**. In turn, each nested template provisions multiple resources. For example, the **Virtual Machines** nested template provisions storage accounts, public IP addresses, network interface cards, and virtual machines, while the **Web App** template provisions Serverfarm, Sites, ConnectionString, AppSettings, Redis Cache, and Traffic Manager Resources:

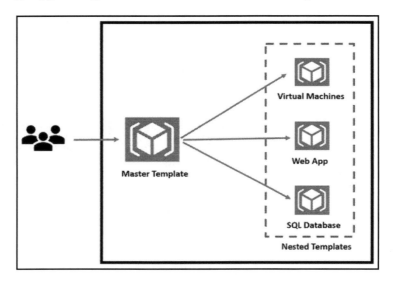

It's now time to look into the implementation of linked templates.

Linked templates should be created and stored within a well-defined URI. Linked templates are no different from normal ARM templates, and they are, by themselves, a complete template. Linked templates accept parameters, provision resources, and generate output.

We will reuse the same template in our upcoming example that we used for provisioning Azure SQL Server, as well as the database used when explaining the `reference` function.

We will name the template `nestedSQLTemplate` and upload it to a storage location within the `templates` container, as shown in the following screenshot:

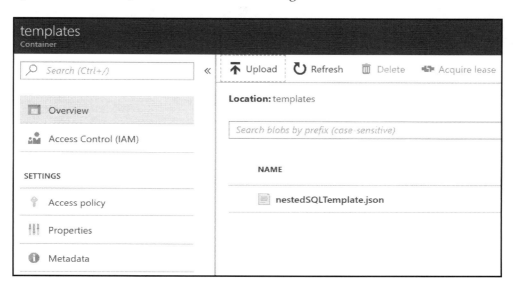

It is important to note that the Azure Storage container hosting nested templates should not have blob or container public access levels enabled. It should be private, and only entities holding valid **Shared Access Signatures** (**SAS**) tokens should be allowed to access the container's contents. Moreover, the holder should only have permission to read the container, not to modify or delete it. In the next image, notice that the **Public access level** is set to **Private** and the **Name** of the container is `templates`:

Understanding Core Elements of ARM Templates

If you have not already generated the SAS token, generate a new token, as shown in the next image. This SAS token, along with the URI of the linked templates, will be used within the master template for invoking the nested template:

The master template will contain `deployment` resources, along with other resources. The `deployment` resource is responsible for invoking linked templates and are similar to other resources in all aspects; the only difference is that it invokes other templates to create resources. The `deployment` resource also has its own set of properties. These properties include a `mode` property that can take `Incremental` or `complete` as its value, a `templateLink` property that points to a valid URI of a linked template, and a `contentVersion` property to determine the version of a linked ARM template. It also has a `parameters` section that is used to supply `parameters` to a nested template. The `parameters` used by the master and linked templates should match in terms of data types, as shown in the following example:

```
{
    "type": "Microsoft.Resources/deployments",
    "apiVersion": "2017-05-10",
    "name": "DeploySQLResources",
```

```
        "properties": {
          "mode": "Incremental",
          "templateLink": {
            "uri": "[variables('completeNestedTemplateURL')]",
            "contentVersion": "1.0.0.0"
          },
          "parameters": {
            "sqlServerName": {
              "value": "[parameters('sqlServerName')]"
            },
            "sqlServerAdministratorLoginName": {
              "value": "[parameters('sqlServerAdministratorLoginName')]"
            },
            "sqlServerAdministratorLoginPassword": {
              "value": "[parameters('sqlServerAdministratorLoginPassword')]"
            },
          }
        }
      }
```

As well as the properties discussed previously, a number of additional properties were recently added to the `deployment` resource. These include `subscriptionId` and `resourceGroup`, explained as follows:

- The `subscriptionId` property is used to deploy the template in a different subscription to the one used for deployment. This helps to deploy linked templates and their contained resources to different subscriptions from within a single ARM template and deployment.
- The `resourceGroup` property is used to deploy the template in a different target resource group to the one used for deployment. This helps to deploy linked templates and their contained resources to a different resource group from within a single ARM template and deployment.

The following section explains the code required to create a master template that's responsible for invoking a linked template. The example will use the code in `chapter-3 - listing 4.txt` as a linked template.

The code for the entire template is available in the `chapter-3 - listing5.txt` file from the accompanying chapter code.

The `parameters` section of the master ARM template accepts parameters related to Azure SQL. These `parameters` are shown in the following code listing. The template takes `parameters` relating to the SQL Server name, username, password, database name, database edition, collation, size, and service objective SKU. These parameter values will then be supplied to the linked template. Notice that the password is of the `secureString` type:

```
"parameters": {
    "sqlServerName": {
        "type": "string"
    },
    "sqlServerAdministratorLoginName": {
        "type": "string"
    },
    "sqlServerAdministratorLoginPassword": {
        "type": "securestring"
    },
    "sqlDatabaseCollation": {
        "type": "string",
        "defaultValue": "SQL_Latin1_General_CP1_CI_AS"
    },
    "sqlDatabaseEdition": {
        "type": "string",
        "defaultValue": "Standard"
    },
    "sqlDatabaseMaxSizeBytes": {
        "type": "string",
        "defaultValue": "107374182400"
    },
    "sqlDatabaseName": {
        "type": "string"
    },
    "sqlDatabaseRequestedServiceObjectiveName": {
        "type": "string",
        "defaultValue": "S2"
    }
}
```

The preceding template defines a number of variables that work together to form the complete URI needed to invoke the linked templates. Note that the SAS token is declared within the template and appended to the end of the linked template URI. In Chapter 7, *Design Patterns*, we will create another ARM template that will store this SAS token within the Azure Key vault, from where the ARM template can access information, as outlined in the following example:

```
"variables" : {

 "storagekey":
"?sv=2017-11-09&ss=bfqt&srt=sco&sp=rwdlacup&se=2018-08-20T19:22:51Z&st=2018
-08-20T11:22:51Z&spr=https&sig=4oGQeTncirZHxyyiMv%2Bhx1A4Tmx7%2FF4Xbp64i9AT
pd4%3D",

 "nestedTemplateLocation":
"https://sta2usc1esvpnvhddev.blob.core.windows.net/templates/nestedSQLTempl
ate.json",

 "completeNestedTemplateURL": "[concat(variables('nestedTemplateLocation'),
variables('storagekey'))]"
}
```

As you can see, after `variables`, the `resources` section contains a single resource of the `deployment` type. This resource invokes the linked template and sends the necessary `parameters` via linked templates, as follows:

```
{
"type": "Microsoft.Resources/deployments",
"apiVersion": "2017-05-10",
"name": "DeploySQLResources",
"properties": {
    "mode": "Incremental",
    "templateLink": {
        "uri": "[variables('completeNestedTemplateURL')]",
        "contentVersion": "1.0.0.0"
        },
    "parameters": {
        "sqlServerName": {
            "value": "[parameters('sqlServerName')]"
            },
        "sqlServerAdministratorLoginName": {
            "value": "[parameters('sqlServerAdministratorLoginName')]"
            },
        "sqlServerAdministratorLoginPassword": {
            "value": "[parameters('sqlServerAdministratorLoginPassword')]"
            },
        "sqlDatabaseCollation": {
```

```
                "value": "[parameters('sqlDatabaseCollation')]"
            },
            "sqlDatabaseEdition": {
                "value": "[parameters('sqlDatabaseEdition')]"
            },
            "sqlDatabaseMaxSizeBytes": {
                "value": "[parameters('sqlDatabaseMaxSizeBytes')]"
            },
            "sqlDatabaseName": {
                "value": "[parameters('sqlDatabaseName')]"
            },
            "sqlDatabaseRequestedServiceObjectiveName": {
                "value": "[parameters('sqlDatabaseRequestedServiceObjectiveName')]"
            }
        }
    }
}
```

The last section of the template consists of `outputs` section, as shown in the following snippet:

```
"outputs": {
 "DatabaseResourceID": {
     "type": "string",
     "value": "[reference('DeploySQLResources').outputs.SQLDatabaseResourceIDfromDiffernetSubscription.value]"
     },
 "SQLDatabaseObject": {
     "type": "object",
     "value": "[reference('DeploySQLResources').outputs.SQLDatabase.value]"
     },
 "SQLServerObject": {
     "type": "object",
     "value": "[reference('DeploySQLResources').outputs.SQLServer.value]"
     },
 "SQLServerDomain": {
     "type": "string",
     "value": "[reference('DeploySQLResources').outputs.SQLServer1.value]"
     }
 }
```

Nested templates

Nested templates are similar in nature to linked templates. Just as linked templates allow the execution of a separate template from the master template, nested templates help to execute others. However, there are notable differences between the two types.

While linked templates are separate templates and thus stored separately, nested templates are instead defined within the same master template file. While linked templates should be available at a well-defined URI accessible to the master template, there is no such requirement for a nested template. In addition, linked templates should be protected from unauthorized access, while nested templates need not.

However, there are certain constraints to consider before working with nested templates. For example, nested templates do not have the ability to define their own parameters; nor do they return any values using the template's output feature. Nested templates can still access the parameters and variables available at a parent template level, however.

So, what does a nested template look like? We'll show you using an example.

In this example, we will be provisioning two service bus namespaces using a single ARM template. The first service bus namespace, or the primary namespace, will be provisioned just like any other resource and will also be declared at the top level in the resources section. The second service bus namespace, or secondary namespace, will be provisioned through a nested template.

The code for this entire template is available in the `chapter-3 - listing 6.txt` file with the accompanying chapter code.

The following template takes four parameters—two parameters for each service bus namespace. The first parameter defines the namespace, while the second parameter determines the namespace SKU. There are parameters for both the primary and secondary service bus namespace, as shown in the following example:

```
"parameters": {
    "primaryServiceBusNamespaceName": {
      "type": "string",
      "metadata": {
        "description": "Service Bus namespace name"
      }
    },
    "primaryServiceBusSku": {
      "type": "string",
      "metadata": {
        "description": "Service bus SKU"
      }
```

Understanding Core Elements of ARM Templates

```
    },
    "secondaryServiceBusNamespaceName": {
      "type": "string",
      "metadata": {
        "description": "Service Bus namespace name"
      }
    },
    "secondaryServiceBusSku": {
      "type": "string",
      "metadata": {
        "description": "Service bus SKU"
      }
    }
  }
}
```

Within the `resource` section, we have two resources. The primary service bus namespace, `Microsoft.ServiceBus/namespaces`, is declared as top-level resource as shown in the following code. It uses the first two parameters from the `parameters` section. The location is decided based on the resource group region:

```
{
  "apiVersion": "2017-04-01",
  "name": "[parameters('primaryServiceBusNamespaceName')]",
  "type": "Microsoft.ServiceBus/namespaces",
  "location": "[resourceGroup().location]",
  "sku": {
    "name": "[parameters('primaryServiceBusSku')]"
  }
}
```

The second resource in this template is of `Microsoft.Resources/deployments` type. This resource type can invoke both linked as well as nested templates. It contains the definition of an entire template within its `properties` section, as shown in next code listing. Notice that both the `parameters` and `outputs` sections are missing in the nested template, although this restriction may be lifted in the future. The following code lists the two parameters relating to the secondary service bus namespace:

```
{
    "apiVersion": "2018-01-01",
    "name": "nestedTemplate",
    "type": "Microsoft.Resources/deployments",
    "dependsOn": [
      "[concat('Microsoft.Network/networkInterfaces/', variables('nicName'))]"
    ],
    "properties": {
      "mode": "Incremental",
```

```
        "template": {
          "$schema":
"https://schema.management.azure.com/schemas/2015-01-01/deploymentTemplate.json#",
          "contentVersion": "1.0.0.0",
          "resources": [
            {
              "apiVersion": "2017-04-01",
              "name": "[parameters('secondaryServiceBusNamespaceName')]",
              "type": "Microsoft.ServiceBus/namespaces",
              "location": "[resourceGroup().location]",
              "sku": {
                "name": "[parameters('secondaryServiceBusSku')]"
              }
            }
          ]
        }
      }
    }
```

Nested templates are especially useful when you do not want to maintain separate ARM template files, but still, want to define resources separately. Further advantages of nested templates are discussed in greater depth in `Chapter 7`, *Design Patterns*.

Within an ARM template, it is not possible to have two resources with the same name and type; you cannot have two virtual networks with the same name in the same template. However, there are still cases where we might need to declare the same resource twice, and this is where nested templates are useful. Readers should refer to `Chapter 7`, *Design Patterns*, for more detail.

Summary

This brings us to the end of Chapter 3. This chapter laid the foundations for writing more complex ARM templates, which we'll cover in subsequent chapters. It discussed in detail the `resources` and `outputs` sections of templates, expressions, and functions, including `references` and `resourceId`. We also looked into dependency definition and how to create and deploy linked templates.

In the next chapter, we will further build on the concepts explained in this chapter, such as deploying multiple resources using `copy` functions, conditional deployment, and nested templates.

Advance Template Features

In this chapter, we'll discuss relatively advanced topics, compared to the previous chapters. ARM templates can be both simple and difficult for an author. This is because there is no user interface that can generate the code for ARM templates; no drag-and-drop feature that can adjust dependencies between resources, and no wizards that can generate expressions. Things become a bit more convoluted when a single deployment might contain multiple templates linked together.

In this chapter, we will continue using the deployment resource to deploy templates stored in an Azure Storage account. We will also see nested templates, otherwise known as **in-place deployment templates**. Some of the advanced concepts related to deploying resources across resource groups and subscriptions will also be covered as part of this chapter. We will cover looping in ARM templates, using `copy` and `copyIndex` functions. Apart from these advanced ARM template topics, we will also create a complex expression consisting of statements and functions. These expressions are evaluated at runtime, during the deployment of the ARM template.

We will specifically cover the following:

- Creating multiple instances of a resource type
- Creating multiple instances of a resource type using Serial mode
- Creating multiple instances of a resource property
- Using copy to generate multiple variables
- Conditions in ARM templates
- Advance deployments

Creating multiple instances of a resource type

There are times when multiple instances of the same resource type are needed—for example: creating multiple virtual machines, multiple databases, bus service queues, and so on. Although it is possible to code the same resource type multiple times one after another with different names, it is definitely not the best way to author ARM templates for provisioning multiple instances of the same resource type.

The ARM template provides a `copy` feature that can be used to loop over any resource type. Later in the chapter, we will see how to loop over resource properties as well. Apart from the `copy` element, ARM templates provide a few other functions that help with creating expressions, enabling looping for resources. These functions are `copy` and `copyindex`.

A `copy` element comprises four properties, as shown here:

```
"copy": {
    "name": "name of copy object",
    "count": "integer value and number of times the copy object should loop",
    "mode": "provision resource in 'parallel' or 'serial'",
    "batchSize": "integer value and the size for each serial execution"
},
```

The `copy` object is part of the resource itself. Each `copy` object has a unique property name within the template. The name has special importance, because it not only acts as an identifier for the `copy` object, but it's also used for referencing and establishing dependencies between the resources from other parts of the template. Let's discuss the properties:

- The count property of the `copy` object refers to the number of times the `copy` object should loop over the entire resource. It is of the integer data type.
- The mode property can take either `serial` or `parallel` as its value. The mode is by default assigned a `parallel` value. Parallel execution means that all resources are provisioned in parallel. For example, if a resource should be created five times, they all are created in parallel. If there needs to be a parallel execution, it is difficult to ascertain which resource out of all these resources will be created first. Serial is the opposite of parallel because the resources are created one after another, in sequence.

- The `batchSize` is used in conjunction with the `Serial` mode value. While creating resources in `Serial` mode, this number signifies the number of resources that should be created as a group.

Here's an example of a `copy` element within a resource:

```
"copy": {
  "name": "keyVaults",
  "count": "[length(parameters('Locations'))]",
  "mode": "Serial",
  "batchSize": 2
},
```

An important function that helps to make looping work is the `copyindex` function. We all know that `copy` helps with iterating over the same resource type, to create multiple instances. This function helps with retrieving the current iteration value. By default, the `copyindex` function starts at 0 and gets incremented by 1 with every iteration.

As we all know by now, the names of resources within an ARM template should be unique. While looping using the `copy` object, every time the resource loops, the name for the new resource should be different than the previous one. To create a unique resource name, the current value of this function can be appended to the name. This will ensure that new resources with unique names are generated.

Let's understand the usage of `copy` and `copyindex`, with the help of an example. In this example, we will provide a couple of storage accounts, using an ARM template. Within the ARM template, there will be just a single definition of a storage account; however, using the `copy` element, multiple resource instances will be created. The entire code for this ARM template is available with the chapter-accompanied code file: `chapter-4 - listing1.txt`.

The parameters for this ARM template are shown next. There is just a single parameter that accepts the name of a storage account. It is of the `string` data type, and the minimum length of the value is 5:

```
"parameters": {
    "storageAccountName" : {"type": "string", "minLength": 5}
}
```

Advance Template Features

The `variables` section of the ARM template is shown next. It declares a single variable, and it ensures that the value of a storage account is unique, by concatenating the storage name parameter with a unique string generated by the `uniqueString` function:

```
"variables": {
    "storageAccountNameVar":
"[tolower(concat(parameters('storageAccountName'),
uniqueString(resourceGroup().id)))]"
 }
```

Next, we come to the `resources` section. As mentioned before, the section contains just one resource of type `Microsoft.Storage/storageAccounts`. This resource contains a `copy` element that is configured to run twice. The names of storage accounts are not static; instead, they are determined using expressions and functions. As discussed earlier, the name of the storage account should be unique within the ARM template, so the `copyindex` function is used to retrieve the current iteration count and append that count to the storage account's name.

You should note that the storage account name is a unique resource, in terms that its name should not only be unique within the ARM template but globally as well. The initial value for the storage account name comes from the variable section, and the value from the `copyindex` function is concatenated to it, to generate a unique name. The first time the `copy` iterates, the value of `copyindex` is 0 by default, and the next time it would be 1:

```
"resources": [
    {
    "apiVersion": "2018-02-01",
    "name": "[concat(variables('storageAccountNameVar'), copyindex())]",
    "location": "[resourceGroup().location]",
    "type": "Microsoft.Storage/storageAccounts",
    "sku": {
        "name": "Standard_LRS"
        },
    "copy": {
        "name": "storages",
        "count": 2
        },
    "kind": "StorageV2",
    "properties": {
        "encryption": {
            "services": {
                "blob": {
                    "enabled": true
                    },
                "file": null
                },
```

```
            "keySource": "Microsoft.Storage"
          }
        }
      }
    ]
```

It should be noted that the default starting value of the `copyindex` function can be changed from 0 to another value by passing the new value as its parameter, as shown next. It is also to be noted that the storage accounts are created in parallel, since the mode is `parallel` by default:

```
copyindex(1)
```

In this case, the starting value of `copyindex` is 1 rather than 0.

The default `copy` mode is parallel, and so the storage accounts are provisioned in parallel.

Creating multiple instances of a resource type, using Serial mode

In the previous section, we showed an example of parallel resource execution. In this section, we'll see how the same `resources` can be executed and provisioned in parallel. The parameters and variables section is the same as it was in the last example.

The `resources` section is shown next. The only difference in this example compared to the previous one is that the `copy` element is using `Serial` as the mode property value, which ensures that storage accounts are created one after another. The entire code for this ARM template is available with a chapter-accompanied code file: `chapter-4 - listing2.txt`:

```
    "resources": [
      {
        "apiVersion": "2018-02-01",
        "name": "[concat(variables('storageAccountNameVar'), copyindex())]",
        "location": "[resourceGroup().location]",
        "type": "Microsoft.Storage/storageAccounts",
        "sku": {
          "name": "Standard_LRS"
        },
        "copy": {
          "name": "storages",
          "count": 2,
          "mode": "Serial"
        },
```

```
      "kind": "StorageV2",
      "properties": {
        "encryption": {
          "services": {
            "blob": {
              "enabled": true
            },
            "file": null
          },
          "keySource": "Microsoft.Storage"
        }
      }
    }
  ]
}
```

Creating multiple instances of a resource property

When ARM templates were launched for the first time, they were not feature-rich. It was extremely difficult to iterate and create multiple properties for a resource, since `copy` was only supported at resource level. The `copy` element could not be used for the properties of a resource. This has changed over the years, with the addition of new capabilities within ARM templates. Recently, ARM templates added the capability to loop over resource properties, using the `copy` element.

You should note the special syntax for the `copyIndex()` function when used alongside property iterations. The `copyIndex` function takes the name of the copy iteration to distinguish it from the resource-level `copyIndex` function. Remember, we can have a `copy` iteration at the resource level and multiple `copy` iterations at the property level. To distinguish between these `copy` iterators, the name should be supplied as a parameter to the `copyIndex` function.

The next example is about creating multiple data disks for a virtual machine. Virtual machines can have more than one data disk, and it is a common requirement to create multiple data disks during the provisioning of a virtual machine. The entire code for this ARM template is available with the chapter- accompanied code file: `chapter-4 - listing3.json`:

```
{
  "name": "examplevm",
  "type": "Microsoft.Compute/virtualMachines",
```

```
      "apiVersion": "2017-03-30",
      "properties": {
        "storageProfile": {
          "copy": [
            {
              "name": "dataDisks",
              "count": 3,
              "input": {
                "lun": "[copyIndex('dataDisks')]",
                "createOption": "Empty",
                "diskSizeGB": "1023",
                "name": "[concat(variables('vmName'), '-datadisk', copyIndex('dataDisks'))]"
              }
            }
          ]
        }
      }
    }
```

This will result in the following output. Readers should notice how the copy element generated multiple JSON objects, which are separated by commas. The name property in the copy element became the variable name and was assigned an array comprising of all the newly generated JSON objects:

```
{
  "name": "examplevm",
  "type": "Microsoft.Compute/virtualMachines",
  "apiVersion": "2017-03-30",
  "properties": {
    "storageProfile": {
      "dataDisks": [
        {
          "lun": 0,
          "createOption": "Empty",
          "diskSizeGB": "1023",
          "name" : "MyWindowsVM-datadisk0"
        },
        {
          "lun": 1,
          "createOption": "Empty",
          "diskSizeGB": "1023",
          "name" : "MyWindowsVM-datadisk1"
        },
        {
          "lun": 2,
          "createOption": "Empty",
          "diskSizeGB": "1023",
```

```
            "name" : "MyWindowsVM-datadisk2"
          }
        ]
      }
    }
}
```

Using copy to generate multiple variables

It is also possible to generate multiple variables at runtime using the `copy` object. There are times when multiple variables are required and the count and values for them are not known at the time of design. The number of variables and their values is known only during deployment time.

For example, creating multiple subnets for virtual networks based on user inputs is related to its `count`, `name`, and `values`. We could create few variables for subnet names, but we can never be certain about them, since the count is dynamic. Instead of declaring each one separately, it is possible to generate those variables using the `copy` object.

The example shown next generates an array comprising multiple JSON objects, each in turn comprising multiple properties. Only the `variables` section is shown here from the code perspective. It creates an array of virtual directories that can be used to configure Azure Web Apps. The entire code for this ARM template is available with chapter-accompanied code file: `chapter-4 - listing4.txt`:

```
     "variables": {
       "virtualPath": [
         "/myapp/api",
         "/myapp/api/internal/login"
       ],
       "physicalPath": [
         "site\\wwwroot\\armwebsite",
         "site\\wwwroot\\armwebsite\\internal\\login"
       ],
       "copy": [
         {
           "name": "virtualDirectories",
           "count": "[length(variables('physicalPath'))]",
           "input": {
             "virtualPath":
"[variables('virtualPath')[copyIndex('virtualDirectories')]]",
             "physicalPath":
"[variables('physicalPath')[copyIndex('virtualDirectories')]]",
             "preloadEnabled": false,
```

```
            "virtualDirectories": null
        }
      }
    ]
}
```

This template consists of three variables: `virtualPath`, `physicalPath`, and `virtualDirectories`. Each of them is a type of array. The `copy` object is a runtime object, and when it gets executed, it generates the `virtualDirectories` variable of the array type. It consists of a number of items dependent on the `physicalPath` array variable. It iterates over and generates an object consisting of four properties: `virtualPath`, `physicalPath`, `preloadEnabled`, and `virtualDirectories`.

Let's execute this template, using the PowerShell `cmdlet`:

```
New-AzureRmResourceGroupDeployment -Name "test1" -ResourceGroupName
"testrg" -TemplateFile "C:\Users\rites\Desktop\A - Chapter5\chapter-4 -
listing4.json"  -Mode Incremental -Verbose
```

The result is as follows:

```
Outputs        :
                 Name              Type                        Value
                 ===============   ========================    ==========
                 arrayOutput       Array                       [
                   {
                     "virtualPath": "/myapp/api",
                     "physicalPath": "site\\wwwroot\\armwebsite",
                     "preloadEnabled": false,
                     "virtualDirectories": null
                   },
                   {
                     "virtualPath": "/myapp/api/internal/login",
                     "physicalPath": "site\\wwwroot\\armwebsite\\internal\\login",
                     "preloadEnabled": false,
                     "virtualDirectories": null
                   },
                   {
                     "virtualPath": "/myapp/api/external/login",
                     "physicalPath": "site\\wwwroot\\armwebsite\\internal\\login",
                     "preloadEnabled": false,
                     "virtualDirectories": null
                   }
                 ]
```

Advance Template Features

The result comprises an array of multiple objects with values from the `physicalPath` and the `virtualPath` array variables.

It is also possible to generate a JSON object comprising of multiple array objects, using the syntax shown next. The entire code for this ARM template is available with the chapter-accompanied code file: `chapter-4 - listing5.txt`. In the next code listing, there are two arrays defined—`virtualPath` and `physicalPath`. Using the `copy` elements, both these arrays are combined, to generate JSON objects:

```
      "variables": {
        "virtualPath": [
          "/myapp/api",
          "/myapp/api/internal/login",
          "/myapp/api/external/login"
        ],
        "physicalPath": [
          "site\\wwwroot\\armwebsite",
          "site\\wwwroot\\armwebsite\\internal\\login",
          "site\\wwwroot\\armwebsite\\internal\\login"
        ],
        "myVirtualDirectories": {
          "copy": [
            {
              "name": "virtualDirectories",
              "count": "[length(variables('physicalPath'))]",
              "input": {
                "virtualPath":
 "[variables('virtualPath')[copyIndex('virtualDirectories')]]",
                "physicalPath":
 "[variables('physicalPath')[copyIndex('virtualDirectories')]]",
                "preloadEnabled": false,
                "virtualDirectories": null
              }
            }
          ]
        }
      }
```

The output from this template is as follows:

```
Outputs       :
                Name            Type                        Value
                =============   =========================   =========
                arrayOutput     Object                      {
                  "virtualDirectories": [
                    {
                      "virtualPath": "/myapp/api",
                      "physicalPath": "site\\wwwroot\\armwebsite",
                      "preloadEnabled": false,
                      "virtualDirectories": null
                    },
                    {
                      "virtualPath": "/myapp/api/internal/login",
                      "physicalPath": "site\\wwwroot\\armwebsite\\internal\\login",
                      "preloadEnabled": false,
                      "virtualDirectories": null
                    },
                    {
                      "virtualPath": "/myapp/api/external/login",
                      "physicalPath": "site\\wwwroot\\armwebsite\\internal\\login",
                      "preloadEnabled": false,
                      "virtualDirectories": null
                    }
                  ]
                }
```

Conditions in ARM templates

In earlier versions of ARM templates, there was no provision of using `if...else` conditional statements. During the Build 2018 event, new functions were released to ARM templates, and the `conditions` feature was one of those functions. There are times when a resource should be provisioned based on a condition. For example, a resource should be conditionally provisioned, based on a parameter value of `true` only.

ARM templates provide multiple comparison functions such as `equals`, `greater`, `greaterOrEquals`, `less`, and `lessOrEquals` that are self-explanatory and used in conjunction with the `if` logical function.

There are also other logical functions such as `and`, `or`, and `not` available in ARM templates, and they can be combined with comparison functions, to create dynamic conditional expressions.

Conditions can be authored in two ways in ARM templates:

- Conditions that return a Boolean value
- Conditions that return any data type

Conditions that return a Boolean value

Resources can be deployed based on a conditional expression. If the expression evaluates to `true`, the resource is deployed; otherwise, it's not. Every resource has a condition property, and it can be used to evaluate the expression.

In the next example, the storage resource has a condition property, and its value is an expression that will evaluate to either true or false. The resource is deployed when the expression evaluates to true.

The expression `[equals(mod(copyindex(),2),1)]` uses the `equals` function to evaluate whether the modulus obtained by dividing the `copyindex` function results in 1. If it results in 1, true is returned, otherwise false is. Astute readers might have already found that this expression will evaluate to true for odd numbers and false for even numbers. It means the storage account will be created only for odd numbers in `copyindex`. The entire code for this ARM template is available with the chapter- accompanied code file: `chapter-4 - listing6.txt`.

The code contains a single parameter related to the storage account name, as shown next:

```
"parameters": {
  "storageAccountName": {
    "type": "string",
    "minLength": 5
  }
},
```

The code also declares just a single variable, to ensure the name of the storage account is all in lowercase and it is unique within the Azure DNS names related to the storage account:

```
"variables": {
  "storageAccountNameVar":
"[tolower(concat(parameters('storageAccountName'),
uniqueString(resourceGroup().id)))]"
},
```

There is a single resource in this template. This resource provisions multiple Azure Storage Accounts because of the `copy` iterator used within the resource definition. It is important to note the `condition` property in this resource definition. The value of this property determines whether the resource should be provisioned. The value assigned to this property is an expression that evaluates for equality between two values.

The first value is the remainder obtained after dividing the current iteration by 2, and the second value is 1. The remainder obtained by dividing a number by 2 will result in a value that is either 0 or 1. If the remainder is 0, the current iteration value is even; otherwise, it is odd. When the copy iterator iterates over this resource type, the conditional statement will be evaluated once per iteration. During the evaluation, it checks whether the current iteration number is an odd number, and only if it is an odd number is the storage account created:

```
"resources": [
    {
        "condition": "[equals(mod(copyindex(),2),1)]",
        "apiVersion": "2018-02-01",
        "name": "[concat(variables('storageAccountNameVar'), copyindex())]",
        "location": "[resourceGroup().location]",
        "type": "Microsoft.Storage/storageAccounts",
        "sku": {   "name": "Standard_LRS" },
        "copy": {
          "name": "storages",
          "count": 4
        },
        "kind": "StorageV2",
        "properties": {
          "encryption": {
            "services": {
              "blob": { "enabled": true },
              "file": null
            },
            "keySource": "Microsoft.Storage"
          }
        }
    }
]
```

Conditions that return condition values

ARM templates provide an `if` function that returns values conditionally, depending on whether the given left condition matches the value on the right. The value returned could be of any JSON-supported data type. This means that it can also return Boolean values, as shown in previous example code, or other values, such as `string`, `integer`, `object`, `array`, `secureString`, and `secureObject`. The `if` function has a syntax, as shown next:

```
if ( <<condition>>, <<return this value if condition is true>>, <<return this value if condition is false>> )
```

Advance Template Features

If we were to rewrite the conditional expression used in the previous example, using the `if` function, it could be written as shown here:

```
"condition": "[bool(if(equals(mod(copyindex(),2),1), 'true', 'false'))]",
```

The `if` function is especially useful for assigning values to resource properties. In the next example, two additional properties are added: `HighDurability` and `isVersion2`. Both of these parameters are used in the `if` loop for evaluating conditions. The `HighDurability` parameter is used to determine the storage account's SKU. If the `HighDurability` is true, then premium storage is provisioned; otherwise, standard storage is provisioned. Similarly, the `isVersion2` parameter decides the version of the storage account. If it's true, then `version2` of the storage account is provisioned; otherwise, it will be `version1`.

The entire code for this ARM template is available with the chapter-accompanied code file: `chapter-4 - listing7.txt`. The template has three parameters defined related to the storage account name, whether premium storage should be provisioned, and the version of the storage account. This is displayed here:

```
"parameters": {
    "storageAccountName": {
      "type": "string",
      "minLength": 5
    },
    "HighDurability": {
      "type": "string",
      "defaultValue": "true"
    },
    "isVersion2": {
      "type": "string",
      "defaultValue": "false"
    }
},
```

The preceding code also declares just a single variable, to ensure the name of storage account is all in lowercase, and it is unique within the Azure DNS names related to the storage account:

```
"variables": {
   "storageAccountNameVar":
 "[tolower(concat(parameters('storageAccountName'),
 uniqueString(resourceGroup().id)))]"
   },
```

The `resources` section contains a single resource, similar to the one used in the previous example.

However, there is a difference in its configuration as well. The difference is the `name` property of the SKU object and the `kind` property value. Both of these properties are using conditional `if` statements, and values assigned to these properties are determined based on the values sent to the parameters while deploying the template:

```
    "resources": [
      {
        "condition": "[equals(mod(copyindex(),2),1)]",
        "apiVersion": "2018-02-01",
        "name": "[concat(variables('storageAccountNameVar'), copyindex())]",
        "location": "[resourceGroup().location]",
        "type": "Microsoft.Storage/storageAccounts",
        "sku": {
          "name": "[concat(  if(equals(parameters('HighDurability'), 'true'), 'Premium_LRS','Standard_GRS') )]"
        },
        "copy": {
          "name": "storages",
          "count": 4
        },
        "kind": "[concat(  if(equals(parameters('isVersion2'), 'true'), 'StorageV2','Storage') )]",
        "properties": {
          "encryption": {
            "services": {
              "blob": { "enabled": true  },
              "file": null
            },
            "keySource": "Microsoft.Storage"
          }
        }
      }
    ]
```

Advanced deployments

In the last chapter, we introduced deployments, using multiple templates. Resources can be defined within multiple ARM templates, and these ARM templates can be weaved together to create a complete deployment solution. Chapter 3, *Understanding Core Elements of ARM Templates*, introduced linked and nested templates and explained the process of composing multiple templates together. As we know, the ARM template provides a resource type named deployment; in this section, we will investigate some of the advanced features of the deployment resource and also expand our knowledge of linked and nested templates from the previous chapter.

Using copy with deployment resources

The `copy` object can be used to iterate over the deployment resource type as well as create multiple deployments. The deployment is linked to another ARM template, and, as a result, the linked ARM templates is called **multiple times** and it **provisions multiple resources**.

It is important to understand that when a `deployment` resource is executed, it creates a separate deployment rather than provisioning resources within the same deployment.

For executing multiple subdeployments using ARM templates, we need a linked template, and we will use the template shown in the following code block. The entire code for this ARM template is available with the chapter-accompanied code file: `chapter-4 - listing8.txt`. It is the same template that we have used in the last two sections.

This template should be uploaded to a storage account, and the URL of that template should be used in the deployment resource. The name of the storage account used in this example is `myarmtemplates`, and the `name` of the linked ARM template is `chapter-4 - listing8.txt`. A `copy` object is added to the resource definition that loops twice, and the `copyindex` function in the resource `name` property ensures that we do not have multiple resource instances with the same name. Note that there is no `copy` object within the linked template, where the storage resource is defined. The entire code for this ARM template is available with the chapter-accompanied code file: `chapter-4 - listing9.txt`:

```
{
  "$schema": "https://schema.management.azure.com/schemas/2015-01-01/deploymentTemplate.json#",
  "contentVersion": "1.0.0.0",
  "parameters": {
    "storageAccountName": {
      "type": "string",
      "minLength": 5
    }
  },
  "resources": [
    {
      "apiVersion": "2017-05-10",
      "name": "[concat('nestedTemplate', copyindex())]",
      "type": "Microsoft.Resources/deployments",
      "copy": {
        "name": "looping",
        "count": 2
      },
      "properties": {
```

```
            "mode": "Incremental",
            "templateLink": {
               "uri":
"https://myarmtemplates.blob.core.windows.net/temps/chapter-4-
listing8.json",
               "contentVersion": "1.0.0.0"
            },
            "parameters": {
               "storageAccountName": { "value":
"[parameters('storageAccountName')]" }
            }
         }
      }
   ]}
```

Creating resource groups, using ARM templates

One of the latest additions to the capabilities of ARM templates is resource group creation. In the past, it was not possible to create resource groups using ARM templates. Generally, templates are deployed to a resource group. As of the writing of this chapter, the PowerShell modules are not yet updated to deploy to a subscription instead of a resource group. However, the capability to conduct a deployment at the subscription level is added to Azure CLI. In this section, we will deploy a template that will create multiple resource groups within a subscription. The entire code for this ARM template is available with the chapter-accompanied code file: `chapter-4 - listing10.txt`:

```
{
   "$schema":
"https://schema.management.azure.com/schemas/2015-01-01/deploymentTemplate.json#",
   "contentVersion": "1.0.0.0",
   "parameters": {
      "Locations": {
         "type": "array",
         "defaultValue": [ "east us", "west us" ],
         "metadata": {
            "description": "Deployment locations"
         }
      }
   },
   "variables": {
   },
   "resources": [
      {
         "type": "Microsoft.Resources/resourceGroups",
```

Advance Template Features

```
      "location": "[parameters('Locations')[copyIndex()]]",
      "name": "[concat('location',copyIndex())]",
      "apiVersion": "2018-05-01",
      "copy": {
        "name": "allResourceGroups",
        "count": "[length(parameters('Locations'))]"
      },
      "properties": {}
    }
  ]
}
```

To deploy this template, Azure CLI should be used, as shown next:

```
az login -u <<your username>> -p <<your password>>

az account set --subscription <<your subscription id or subscription name>>

az deployment create --location WestUS --template-file "<<location of above template>>" --verbose
```

Deploying this template will create two resource groups—one in the eastern US and the other in the western US. You should check the way expressions and functions are used to get the count for the resource group provisioning, and use the `copyindex` function to read them, by indexing the parameter of the array type.

Deploying resources into multiple resource groups, using the deployment resource

The deployment resource is quite special and different than other resource types. It has additional properties that are not available to other resource types. These properties help with deploying resources in different resources groups and subscriptions from the same template. In this section, we will see how to deploy resources to multiple resource groups from the same template. In fact, the template will first create a couple of resource groups in different Azure regions and then deploy Azure Key Vaults to those separate resource groups and regions, using the linked template.

For this example, we need a template that can provision the Azure Key Vault for us. The template shown next creates a Key Vault. This template will be linked to a master template that will pass on the required parameters to create a Key Vault.

The Key Vault template is available with the chapter-accompanied code file: `chapter-4 - listing11.txt`.

The code contains quite a few `parameters` related to Key Vault configuration, as shown next:

```
parameters": {
    "clientId": { "type": "string" },
    "tenantId": { "type": "string" },
    "enabledForDeployment": { "type": "string" },
    "enabledForTemplateDeployment": { "type": "string" },
    "enableVaultForVolumeEncryption": { "type": "string" },
    "vaultSku": { "type": "string" },
    "vaultName": { "type": "string" },
    "permissions": { "type": "object" }
},
```

There are no variables in this template, and there is a single Azure Key Vault resource defined in the template, as shown next:

```
"resources": [
    {
      "type": "Microsoft.KeyVault/vaults",
      "name": "[concat(parameters('vaultName'), resourceGroup().location)]",
      "apiVersion": "2015-06-01",
      "location": "[resourceGroup().location]",
      "properties": {
        "enabledForDeployment": "[parameters('enabledForDeployment')]",
        "enabledForTemplateDeployment": "[parameters('enabledForTemplateDeployment')]",
        "enabledForVolumeEncryption": "[parameters('enableVaultForVolumeEncryption')]",
        "tenantId": "[parameters('tenantId')]",
        "accessPolicies": [
          {
            "tenantId": "[parameters('tenantId')]",
            "objectId": "[parameters('clientId')]",
            "permissions": "[parameters('permissions')]"
          }
        ],
        "sku": {
          "name": "[parameters('vaultSku')]",
          "family": "A"
        }
      }
    }
],
```

There is a single output from the template, as shown next:

```
"outputs": {
    "keyVaultName": {
      "type": "string",
      "value": "[concat(parameters('vaultName'),resourceGroup().location)]"
    }
}
```

This template should be uploaded to an Azure storage account. This template takes eight parameters needed to configure the Azure Key Vault. I am not going to go into the details of Azure Key Vault configuration; however, readers will notice that important information, such as tenant ID, Object ID (also known as client ID or application ID), permissions, along with a few flags, needs to be supplied to the ARM template.

To have an application ID, we need either an already existing Service Application in the current Azure Active Directory, or we should be creating a new one. An Azure Service Application can be created using Azure Portal, Azure PowerShell, and Azure CLI, and in this example, I will create a Service application using Azure PowerShell. The same Service Application ID will be used as an Object ID or Client ID in ARM templates.

The PowerShell command for creating an Azure Service Application is shown next. The entire code for this PowerShell script is available with the chapter-accompanied code file: `chapter-4 - listing12.txt`. Readers are advised to provide their own values for DisplayName and other parameters.

```
$app = New-AzureRmADApplication -DisplayName "ARMtemplateBook" -IdentifierUris "http://ARMtemplateBook" -ReplyUrls "http://ARMtemplateBook/callback"
```

After creating a Service Application, we create a Service Principal based on it using PowerShell as shown in the next command:

```
$principal = New-AzureRmADServicePrincipal -ApplicationId $app.ApplicationId -Password (ConvertTo-SecureString -String Pa55w0rd -AsPlainText -Force)
```

After the Service Principal is created, the appropriate permissions should be assigned to it so that it has access to resources and it is able to execute tasks on them. This is shown in the next command, which provides the owner role to the newly created Service Principal:

```
$assignment = New-AzureRmRoleAssignment -RoleDefinitionName owner -ServicePrincipalName $app.ApplicationId.Guid
```

The next step is to create a master ARM template that will compose and link the previously authored Azure Key Vault ARM template. In this template, we declare variables for Key Vault and send them to the linked template. The code for this master template is available in this file: chapter-4 - listing13.txt.

The parameters section of this template just takes a single Locations parameter, as shown next:

```
"parameters": {
   "Locations": {
     "type": "array",
     "defaultValue": [ "east us", "west us" ],
     "metadata": {
        "description": "Deployment locations"
     }
   }
}
```

The variables definitions are shown next. They define the configuration values for the Key Vault:

```
"variables": {
  "enabledForDeployment": "true",
  "enabledForTemplateDeployment": "true",
  "enableVaultForVolumeEncryption": "true",
  "tenantId": "xxxxxxxx-xxxx-xxxx-xxxx-xxxxxxxxxxxx",
  "objectId": "5ecc2085-c985-4dec-a4ce-1108a252833b",
  "permissions": {
       "keys": [ "all" ],
       "secrets": [ "all" ]
     },
  "vaultSku": "Standard",
  "vaultName": "myVault"
},
```

There are two resources in this template. The first resource creates multiple resource groups, as shown in the following code:

```
        {
          "type": "Microsoft.Resources/resourceGroups",
          "location": "[parameters('Locations')[copyIndex()]]",
          "name": "[concat('location',copyIndex())]",
          "apiVersion": "2018-05-01",
          "copy": {
            "name": "allResourceGroups",
            "count": "[length(parameters('Locations'))]"
          },
```

Advance Template Features

```
      "properties": {}
    },
```

The second resource definition iterates over the deployment resource multiple times, based on the value of the `count` property. The `count` property gets its value from the length of the supplied `Location` parameter of type array. This resource invokes the linked template multiple times, once for each resource group created earlier and supplies different parameters to it in each iteration:

```
    {
      "apiVersion": "2017-05-10",
      "name": "[concat('nestedTemplate', copyindex())]",
      "type": "Microsoft.Resources/deployments",
      "resourceGroup": "[concat('location',copyIndex())]",
      "copy": {
        "name": "keyVaults",
        "count": "[length(parameters('Locations'))]"
      },
      "dependsOn": [ "allResourceGroups" ],
      "properties": {
        "mode": "Incremental",
        "templateLink": {
          "uri": "https://tempssdfsdf.blob.core.windows.net/temps/Keyvault.json",
          "contentVersion": "1.0.0.0"
        },
        "parameters": {
          "clientId": { "value": "[variables('objectId')]" },
          "tenantId": { "value": "[variables('tenantId')]" },
          "enabledForDeployment": { "value": "[variables('enabledForDeployment')]" },
          "enabledForTemplateDeployment": { "value": "[variables('enabledForTemplateDeployment')]" },
          "enableVaultForVolumeEncryption": { "value": "[variables('enableVaultForVolumeEncryption')]" },
          "vaultSku": { "value": "[variables('vaultSku')]" },
          "vaultName": { "value": "[variables('vaultName')]" },
          "permissions": { "value": "[variables('permissions')]" }
        }
      }
    }
```

Chapter 4

There is a single output from this master template, and it is shown here:

```
"outputs": {
  "keyvaultdetails": { "type": "string",
      "value":
"[reference('nestedTemplate0').outputs.keyVaultName.value]"
    }
  }
```

Note that the permissions property used in this template is an array type, because the linked template expects an array value for this parameter. It will result in an error if any other data type other than array is supplied.

Also, note that the `dependsOn` element within the deployment resource is establishing a dependency on the resource group `copy` object, which is part of another resource. Instead of depending on the resource group type, declaring a dependency on the `copy` object ensures that unless all the resources to be created are part of the `copy` iteration, the dependent resource will not start provisioning. The Azure Key Vault deployment will only start after the entire operation of creating multiple resource groups is complete.

The output of executing the preceding template is as follows:

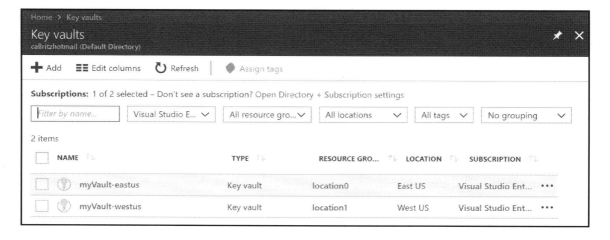

[109]

Deploying resources into multiple resource groups in multiple subscriptions

Apart from deploying resources from the same template to multiple resource groups in multiple regions, it is also possible to deploy in multiple resources groups in multiple subscriptions. The deployments resource has an additional property, `subscriptionid`, that accepts the subscription identifier and can deploy resources to those subscriptions.

Building on the previous example, the following code shows the deployment to multiple resource groups in different subscriptions. The entire code for this ARM template is available with the chapter—accompanied code file: `chapter-4 - listing14.txt`.

This template declares a couple of parameters related to the resource group's location and the Azure subscription ID, as shown here:

```
"parameters": {
  "Locations": {
    "type": "array",
    "defaultValue": [ "east us", "west us" ],
    "metadata": {
      "description": "Deployment locations"
    }
  },
  "subscriptions": {
    "type": "array",
    "defaultValue": [ "xxxxxxxx-xxxx-xxxx-xxxxxxxxxxxx", "xxxxxxxx-xxxx-xxxx-xxxxxxxxxxxx" ],
    "metadata": {
      "description": "subscriptions identifiers"
    }
  }
}
```

The `variables` section declares variables related to the Key Vault configuration. Notice that there is an array value assigned to the `permissions` variable. This is shown here:

```
"variables": {
  "enabledForDeployment": "true",
  "enabledForTemplateDeployment": "true",
  "enableVaultForVolumeEncryption": "true",
  "tenantId": "xxxxxxxx-xxxx-xxxx-xxxx-xxxxxxxxxxxx",
  "objectId": "5ecc2085-c985-4dec-a4ce-1108a252833b",
  "permissions": {
    "keys": [ "all" ],
    "secrets": [ "all" ]
  },
```

```
      "vaultSku": "Standard",
      "vaultName": "myVault"
}
```

The resource section contains a single `Deployment` resource definition that iterates and invokes linked templates multiple times and creates a new Azure Key Vault in a separate subscription, resource group, and region in each iteration. This is shown in the next code listing:

```
      "resources": [
        {
          "apiVersion": "2017-05-10",
          "name": "[concat('nestedTemplate', copyindex())]",
          "type": "Microsoft.Resources/deployments",
          "resourceGroup": "[parameters('location')[copyIndex()]]",
          "subscriptionId": "[parameters('subscriptions')[copyIndex()]]",
          "copy": {
            "name": "keyVaults",
            "count": "[length(parameters('Locations'))]",
            "mode": "Serial",
            "batchSize": 2
          },
          "dependsOn": [ "allResourceGroups" ],
          "properties": {
            "mode": "Incremental",
            "templateLink": {
              "uri":
"https://tempssdfsdf.blob.core.windows.net/temps/Keyvault.json",
              "contentVersion": "1.0.0.0"
            },
            "parameters": {
              "clientId": { "value": "[variables('objectId')]" },
              "tenantId": { "value": "[variables('tenantId')]" },
              "enabledForDeployment": { "value":
"[variables('enabledForDeployment')]" },
              "enabledForTemplateDeployment": { "value":
"[variables('enabledForTemplateDeployment')]" },
              "enableVaultForVolumeEncryption":
{"value":"[variables('enableVaultForVolumeEncryption')]"},
              "vaultSku": { "value": "[variables('vaultSku')]" },
              "vaultName": { "value": "[variables('vaultName')]" },
              "permissions": { "value": "[variables('permissions')]" }
            }
          }
        }
      ],
```

Advance Template Features

The `outputs` section contains a single output, as shown in the next code listing:

```
"outputs": {
    "keyvaultdetails": {
        "type": "string",
        "value": "[reference('nestedTemplate0').outputs.keyVaultName.value]"
    }
}
```

Creating Nested Deployments

So far, we have discussed the details of creating modular ARM templates, using linked deployments and templates. A new feature of ARM templates is to have in-place nested deployments. In this, there is no dependency on the availability of an externally stored ARM template, but a separate template structure is embedded within the master template, by means of the `deployments` resource type.

We'll use the same example used for provisioning Key Vaults in multiple resource groups with an in-place nested template displayed in the following code.

The entire code for this ARM template is available with the chapter-accompanied code file: `chapter-4 - listing15.txt`.

There is a single instance of `parameters` within this ARM template, as shown next:

```
"parameters": {
    "Locations": {
        "type": "array",
        "defaultValue": [ "east us", "west us" ],
        "metadata": {
            "description": "Deployment locations"
        }
    }
},
```

The `variables` definitions are the same as those that were used in the last example. They are shown here again for easy reference:

```
"variables": {
    "enabledForDeployment": "true",
    "enabledForTemplateDeployment": "true",
    "enableVaultForVolumeEncryption": "true",
    "tenantId": "771f1cf4-b1ac-4f2e-ad21-de39ea201e7e",
    "clientId": "5ecc2085-c985-4dec-a4ce-1108a252833b",
    "permissions": {
```

```
    "keys": [ "all" ],
    "secrets": [ "all" ]
},
"vaultSku": "Standard",
"vaultName": "gyftdrj"
},
```

The resources section contains the `resourceGroup` resource that creates multiple resource groups, similar to the last example. Then, there is another deployment resource that again runs within a loop, to create multiple `deployments`, and each deployment is responsible for executing a nested template. The deployment resource configuration is shown here:

```
{
    "apiVersion": "2017-05-10",
    "name": "[concat('nestedTemplate', copyindex())]",
    "type": "Microsoft.Resources/deployments",
    "resourceGroup": "[concat('location',copyIndex())]",
    "copy": {
      "name": "keyVaults",
      "count": "[length(parameters('Locations'))]"
    },
    "dependsOn": [ "allResourceGroups" ],
    "properties": {
      "mode": "Incremental",
    }
}
```

The deployment resource also contains a template property that contains a complete ARM template definition itself. This nested template cannot take any parameters and output any return value. It can, however, consume parameters and variables defined at parent templates. The nested template is shown next:

```
    "template": {
          "$schema":
"https://schema.management.azure.com/schemas/2015-01-01/deploymentTemplate.json#",
          "contentVersion": "1.0.0.0",
          "resources": [
            {
              "type": "Microsoft.KeyVault/vaults",
              "name": "[concat(variables('vaultName'),
string(copyindex()))]",
              "location": "[parameters('Locations')[copyIndex()]]",
              "apiVersion": "2015-06-01",
              "properties": {
                "enabledForDeployment":
"[variables('enabledForDeployment')]",
```

Advance Template Features

```
                    "enabledForTemplateDeployment":
"[variables('enabledForTemplateDeployment')]",
                    "enabledForVolumeEncryption":
[variables('enableVaultForVolumeEncryption')]",
                    "tenantId": "[variables('tenantId')]",
                    "accessPolicies": [
                      {
                        "tenantId": "[variables('tenantId')]",
                        "objectId": "[variables('clientId')]",
                        "permissions": "[variables('permissions')]"
                      }
                    ],
                    "sku": {
                      "name": "[variables('vaultSku')]",
                      "family": "A"
                    }
                  }
                }
              ]
            }
```

In this example, instead of using the `templateLink` in the `deployments` resource, just the template property is used, and it is supplied with an entire template as its value. The advantage of this approach is that it is not dependent on the availability and access to an external template; it is completely self-sufficient. All the rules that apply to externally linked templates are applicable to an in-place nested template; however, there are a few additional constraints related to the usage of `parameters`, `variables`, and return values as part of the `outputs` section. I believe these constraints will be removed in the future by the Azure team.

An important thing to note in the case of in-place deployment templates is that `parameters` and `variables` declared at the master template or the global level can be accessed directly, and they need not be passed to the nested template by means of `parameters`.

Summary

This brings us to the conclusion of this chapter. We discussed lots of advanced concepts and implementation in this chapter. These concepts related to `deployments`, `copy` objects, conditional statements, and complex expressions, and functions that help build real, reusable, modular, and maintainable templates.

In the next chapter, we will further focus on some of the scripting-related resources, especially the custom script extension that has the capability to execute PowerShell and Bash scripts on Linux and Windows. It will also show ways to define resources for consuming the desired state configuration scripts, for configuring environments.

Section 2: ARM Template Advanced Concepts

Section 2 of this book uses the concepts described in *Section 1* to create solutions using ARM templates. These solutions consist of bringing multiple concepts together to form a deployment and create multiple resources on Azure. In this section, apart from creating resources as part of the solution, we will also cover unit testing of templates and utilizing best practices when writing modular and reusable templates. An important element of this is design patterns for writing templates, which will also be covered as part of this section.

This section contains the following chapters:

- `Chapter 5`, *IaaS Solutions Using Templates*
- `Chapter 6`, *Unit Testing ARM Templates*
- `Chapter 7`, *Design Patterns*
- `Chapter 8`, *ARM Template Best Practices*

5
IaaS Solutions Using Templates

So far in this book, we have looked at how to provision resources using different methods such as nested deployments and linked deployments, and how to configure those resources. We know that resources are created and configured at the management control level; generally, an ARM template does not configure the inner workings of a resource. However, there are a few resources that need post-deployment configuration—for example, the configuration of an operating system after a virtual machine has been created in overall environment provision.

Fortunately, ARM templates provide us with enough infrastructure and resources to configure the operating system, as well as deploy and configure applications within virtual machines. So in this chapter, we will focus on how to use ARM templates to configure environments within virtual machines.

In this chapter, we will cover the following topics:

- Configuration inside an Azure virtual machine
- Protecting scripts using SAS tokens
- Using `protectedSettings`
- `CustomScriptExtension` as a separate resource

Configuration inside an Azure virtual machine

Azure ARM templates provide extension resources to configure the inside of a virtual machine. Extensions can be of multiple types; two of the most important extension types are as follows:

- Custom Script Extension
- Desired State Configuration

Extension resources are nested resources within a virtual machine resource. They can be declared as a nested resource within a virtual machine resource, or they can be defined as a stand-alone resource with syntax that establishes the parent-child relationship with its parent virtual machines.

Custom Script Extension helps to execute PowerShell scripts and ensure a Desired State Configuration on virtual machines after they have been created.

These two types of extension provide unlimited possibilities for configuring virtual machines. For example, a Custom Script Extension enables users to download Docker images and create new containers using Docker compose files. It can also be used to provide internet information services, create a new web application, set up custom ports, bind and open relevant firewall ports, download dependent utilities and binaries from NuGet and Chocolatey, and even deploy a web application with a custom connection string to Azure SQL.

So, let's now understand the syntax required for declaring a Custom Script Extension. We'll look at examples of Desired State Configuration later.

Custom Script Extension helps executions in PowerShell as well as bash scripts on both Windows and Linux virtual machines. PowerShell scripts should be made available in a well-defined URI, such as an Azure storage account, so that it can be downloaded by an ARM template provided by the Custom Script Extension resource.

Note that the target virtual machine must have internet and the appropriate network security group rules enabled in order to download PowerShell scripts locally. In addition, there can only be one Custom Script Extension per virtual machine—extensions cannot be run either serially or in parallel on one VM.

The extensions resource, like any other resource, includes the usual name, API version, location, and type properties. Since the extension resource is a child resource of virtual machines, it must declare its dependency using the dependsOn element.

What type of configuration to be deployed and configured is declared within a Custom Script Extension's properties section. In this example, it would be CustomScriptExtension and any supported type, such as DesiredStateConfiguration.

Explanations of each property are as follows:

- publisher: This refers to the resource namespace that provides an extension type
- typeHandlerVersion: This is the version of the server-side API that executes and provisions this resource
- AutoUpgradeMinorVersion: This automatically selects the most recent minor version of the extension type; it is usually a Boolean value and also automatically upgrades the resource where necessary

Settings is one of the most important properties in an extension resource because it's where extension details are configured. The properties within settings are different for every extension type. For example, in a CustomScriptExtension extension, the fileUris and commandtoExecute properties should be configured; however, for the operations management suite extension, the workspace ID should be configured.

fileUris refers to all script files that should be downloaded and executed on a target virtual machine. It accepts an array of PowerShell script URLs. These PowerShell files should be available on an Azure Storage Blob container that is protected by access policy. An SAS token or Azure Storage account key is required to access PowerShell script files.

Since multiple PowerShell scripts can be downloaded on a target virtual machine, the command that executes a PowerShell script should be provided as a value to the commandToExecute property in its entirety. The following example uses the concat function to generate this command, which is then executed on the target virtual machine:

```
{
    "name": "test",
    "type": "extensions",
    "location": "[resourceGroup().location]",
    "apiVersion": "2016-03-30",
    "dependsOn": [
      "[resourceId('Microsoft.Compute/virtualMachines', variables('vmName'))]"
```

IaaS Solutions Using Templates

```
        ],
        "tags": {
          "displayName": "test"
        },
        "properties": {
          "publisher": "Microsoft.Compute",
          "type": "CustomScriptExtension",
          "typeHandlerVersion": "1.4",
          "autoUpgradeMinorVersion": true,
          "settings": {
            "fileUris": [
              "[concat(parameters('_artifactsLocation'), '/', variables('testScriptFolder'), '/', variables('testScriptFileName'), parameters('_artifactsLocationSasToken'))]"
            ],
            "commandToExecute": "[concat('powershell -ExecutionPolicy Unrestricted -File ', variables('testScriptFolder'), '/', variables('testScriptFileName'))]"
          }
        }
      }
```

Let's now focus on how to create a virtual machine and execute a Custom Script Extension so we can install internet information services and check that the worldwide publishing services are up and running.

The PowerShell script takes two parameters, `featureName` and `serviceName`. The feature name is the name of the Windows feature that needs installing, and the service name is the name of the service that should be configured to run automatically, as shown in the following snippet:

```
[CmdletBinding()]
param

(    [Parameter(Mandatory = $true)]
    [string]
    $featureName,   [Parameter(Mandatory = $true)]
    [string]
    $serviceName
)

Install-WindowsFeature -name $featureName -IncludeManagementTools -Verbose
$service = Get-Service -Name $serviceName -ErrorAction Stop

if ($service.StartType -ne 'Automatic')
{
    Write-Verbose -Message "Setting startup type for $serviceName to
```

```
automatic"
    Set-Service -Name $serviceName -StartupType Automatic
}
if ($service.Status -ne 'Running')
{
    Write-Verbose -Message "Starting service $serviceName"
    Start-Service-Name$serviceName
}
```

The PowerShell script is uploaded to a storage account, `armtfiles`, within the container `templates`. The name of the PowerShell script is `Install-IIS.ps1`.

The mapping of `parameters` and `variables` for a PowerShell script file is as follows:

Name in ARM template	Location in ARM template	Value
storageAccountName	Parameter	https://armtfiles.blob.core.windows.net
firstCustomScriptExtensionScriptStorageContainer	Variable	templates
firstCustomScriptExtensionScriptFileName	Variable	install-IIS.ps1

The complete URL of the PowerShell script is `https://armtfiles.blob.core.windows.net/templates/install-IIS.ps1`, which is formed by an expression in the `fileUris` section of the extension, as follows:

```
"[concat(parameters('storageAccountName'), '/',
variables('firstCustomScriptExtensionScriptStorageContainer'), '/',
variables('firstCustomScriptExtensionScriptFileName'))]"
```

The entire code for the extension is as follows:

```
            {
              "name": "firstCustomScriptExtension",
              "type": "extensions",
              "location": "[resourceGroup().location]",
              "apiVersion": "2016-03-30",
              "dependsOn": [
                "[resourceId('Microsoft.Compute/virtualMachines',
variables('vmName'))]"
              ],
              "tags": {
                "displayName": "firstCustomScriptExtension"
              },
              "properties": {
                "publisher": "Microsoft.Compute",
                "type": "CustomScriptExtension",
                "typeHandlerVersion": "1.4",
```

IaaS Solutions Using Templates

```
              "autoUpgradeMinorVersion": true,
              "settings": {
                "fileUris": [
                  "[concat(parameters('storageAccountName'), '/',
variables('firstCustomScriptExtensionScriptStorageContainer'), '/',
variables('firstCustomScriptExtensionScriptFileName'))]"
                ],
                "commandToExecute": "[concat('powershell -ExecutionPolicy
Unrestricted -File ',
variables('firstCustomScriptExtensionScriptFileName'), ' -featureName web-
server -serviceName w3svc')]"
              }
            }
          }
```

The code for creating a virtual machine is not shown in this chapter, however the entire code for the template is available at `WindowsVirtualMachine.json` in the accompanying code of this chapter.

The `variables` section of the code declares a couple of variables relating to Custom Script Extension configuration, shown as follows:

```
        "firstCustomScriptExtensionScriptStorageContainer": "templates",
        "firstCustomScriptExtensionScriptFileName": "install-IIS.ps1"
```

The parameter that accepts the location of the PowerShell script to be executed by the Custom Script Extension is as follows:

```
    "storageAccountName": {
        "type": "string",
        "metadata": {
           "description": "Auto-generated container in staging storage account
to receive post-build staging folder upload"
        }
    }
```

The PowerShell command that deploys the `WindowsVirtualMachine.json` template is shown in the following snippet. Notice how parameters are overridden and sent alongside the execution of `New-AzureRMResourceGroupDeployment` cmdlet:

```
New-AzureRmResourceGroupDeployment -Name "csa01" -ResourceGroupName test01
-Mode Incremental -TemplateFile
"c:\users\rites\source\repos\AzureResourceGroup19\WindowsVirtualMachine.jso
n" -adminUsername "superadmin" -adminPassword $(ConvertTo-SecureString -
String Pa55w0rdPa55w0rd -AsPlainText -Force) -dnsNameForPublicIP
armtemplateunique -storageAccountName
https://armtfiles.blob.core.windows.net -Verbose
```

Protecting scripts using SAS tokens

In the previous example, the PowerShell script was available for download by anyone who possessed its URL. This is not an ideal situation from a security standpoint. The scripts should only be accessible and downloadable by authorized users. Fortunately, the content of an Azure Storage account can be protected by changing its access policy from anonymous access to private access. In such a case, a special token is needed to access the contents of the storage container, as shown in the following screenshot:

IaaS Solutions Using Templates

An SAS token can be generated for any storage account with the necessary permissions for a particular time period, and can also be used in ARM templates to download Custom Script Extensions and PowerShell scripts, as shown in the following screenshot:

The code file `WindowsVirtualMachine-Protected.json` shows the usage of an SAS token within the `CustomScriptExtension` resource.

The only difference between this example and the previous example is the use of an SAS token to access the PowerShell script stored in a protected Azure storage account, as shown in the following snippet:

```
{
        "name": "firstCustomScriptExtension",
        "type": "extensions",
        "location": "[resourceGroup().location]",
        "apiVersion": "2016-03-30",
        "dependsOn": [
          "[resourceId('Microsoft.Compute/virtualMachines', variables('vmName'))]"
        ],
        "tags": {
          "displayName": "firstCustomScriptExtension"
        },
        "properties": {
          "publisher": "Microsoft.Compute",
          "type": "CustomScriptExtension",
          "typeHandlerVersion": "1.4",
          "autoUpgradeMinorVersion": true,
          "settings": {
            "fileUris": [
              "[concat(parameters('storageAccountName'), '/', variables('firstCustomScriptExtensionScriptStorageContainer'), '/', variables('firstCustomScriptExtensionScriptFileName'), parameters('_artifactsLocationSasToken'))]"
            ],
            "commandToExecute": "[concat('powershell -ExecutionPolicy Unrestricted -File ', variables('firstCustomScriptExtensionScriptFileName'), ' -featureName web-server -serviceName w3svc')]"
          }
        }
    }
```

Using protectedSettings

Another way to ensure that data is stored in an encrypted format and is only decrypted on a virtual machine is to use `protectedSettings` along with a Custom Script Extension. This object takes three properties. The configuration of the `CommandToExecute` property is similar to previous configurations; its purpose is to execute PowerShell scripts.

IaaS Solutions Using Templates

The storage account name is where we'll find the PowerShell script stored, and the storage account key will provide the account's access key. This information can be found within the **Access keys** menu item on Azure Portal, as shown in the following screenshot:

When using protected settings, the storage key is provided as its configuration. There is no need to append the SAS token to the URL. The new configuration of the resource is shown in the following snippet. Note that the complete code listing for this example is available the `WindowsVirtualMachine-ProtectedSettings.json` file in the accompanying code of this chapter:

```
{
        "name": "firstCustomScriptExtension",
```

```
            "type": "extensions",
            "location": "[resourceGroup().location]",
            "apiVersion": "2016-03-30",
            "dependsOn": [
                "[resourceId('Microsoft.Compute/virtualMachines', variables('vmName'))]"
            ],
            "tags": {
                "displayName": "firstCustomScriptExtension"
            },
            "properties": {
                "publisher": "Microsoft.Compute",
                "type": "CustomScriptExtension",
                "typeHandlerVersion": "1.4",
                "autoUpgradeMinorVersion": true,
                "settings": {
                    "fileUris": [
                        "[concat(parameters('storageAccountName'), '/', variables('firstCustomScriptExtensionScriptStorageContainer'), '/', variables('firstCustomScriptExtensionScriptFileName'))]"
                    ]
                },
                "protectedSettings": {
                    "commandToExecute": "[concat('powershell -ExecutionPolicy Unrestricted -File ', variables('firstCustomScriptExtensionScriptFileName'), ' -featureName web-server -serviceName w3svc')]",
                    "storageAccountName": "armtfiles",
                    "storageAccountKey": "your key"
                }
            }
        }
```

CustomScriptExtension as separate resource

In all of our previous examples, `CustomScriptExtension` has been a child resource of a virtual machine or created as a nested resource. It is possible, however, to declare the `customscriptextensions` resource as a separate resource outside of a virtual machine. The difference in declaring `customscriptextension` as a separate resource allows you to create reusable modular ARM templates even when the extension resource has been defined in a different ARM template file.

IaaS Solutions Using Templates

While declaring `customscriptextension` as a separate resource, there are changes to be noted in the way both the `name` and `type` properties are assigned. The `name` property should be qualified with the name of the virtual machine, and the `type` property should be a complete property with `virtualmachines` included as part of it.

The following snippet is an example of `customscriptextension` using separate resource definitions. This code is available in the `Seperateresource.json` file in the accompanying chapter code:

```json
{
    "name": "[concat(variables('vmName'),'/','firstCustomScriptExtension')]",
    "type": "Microsoft.Compute/virtualMachines/extensions",
    "location": "[resourceGroup().location]",
    "apiVersion": "2016-03-30",
    "dependsOn": [
      "[resourceId('Microsoft.Compute/virtualMachines', variables('vmName'))]"
    ],
    "tags": {
      "displayName": "firstCustomScriptExtension"
    },
    "properties": {
      "publisher": "Microsoft.Compute",
      "type": "CustomScriptExtension",
      "typeHandlerVersion": "1.4",
      "autoUpgradeMinorVersion": true,
      "settings": {
        "fileUris": [
          "[concat(parameters('storageAccountName'), '/', variables('firstCustomScriptExtensionScriptStorageContainer'), '/', variables('firstCustomScriptExtensionScriptFileName'))]"
        ],
        "commandToExecute": "[concat('powershell -ExecutionPolicy Unrestricted -File ', variables('firstCustomScriptExtensionScriptFileName'), ' -featureName web-server -serviceName w3svc')]"
      }
    }
}
```

Notice the way `name` is defined; it is composed of both the virtual machine name and the extension name. They are concatenated to form the parent-child relationship, as follows:

```
"name": "[concat(variables('vmName'),'/','firstCustomScriptExtension')]",
```

Similarly, check out the way a value is assigned to the `type` property in the following example:

```
"type": "Microsoft.Compute/virtualMachines/extensions",
```

Instead of being just an extension, `type` is fully qualified with parent resources and child types.

Getting output from CustomScriptExtension

There are times when it is important to get relevant information from the output generated by a PowerShell script to know more about the execution and even obtain return values. Luckily, it is possible to read the output of a Custom Script Extension, as shown in the next code listing. In this example, an outputs section has been added, which in turn uses the inbuilt `reference` function to retrieve values from the `customscriptextension` resource. The output from this resource contains properties that help in retrieving the values. The code for this example is available in the `CustomScriptExtension-outputs.json` file in the accompanying chapter code:

```
{
    "name": "[concat(variables('vmName'),'/','firstCustomScriptExtension')]",
    "type": "Microsoft.Compute/virtualMachines/extensions",
    "location": "[resourceGroup().location]",
    "apiVersion": "2016-03-30",
    "dependsOn": [
      "[resourceId('Microsoft.Compute/virtualMachines', variables('vmName'))]"
    ],
    "tags": {
      "displayName": "firstCustomScriptExtension"
    },
    "properties": {
      "publisher": "Microsoft.Compute",
      "type": "CustomScriptExtension",
      "typeHandlerVersion": "1.4",
      "autoUpgradeMinorVersion": true,
      "settings": {
        "fileUris": [
          "[concat(parameters('storageAccountName'), '/', variables('firstCustomScriptExtensionScriptStorageContainer'), '/', variables('firstCustomScriptExtensionScriptFileName'))]"
        ],
        "commandToExecute": "[concat('powershell -ExecutionPolicy Unrestricted -File ',
```

```
        variables('firstCustomScriptExtensionScriptFileName'), ' -featureName web-
        server -serviceName w3svc')]"
                    }
                }
            }
    ],
```

As you can see in the following example, the `outputs` section provides information about the messages generated by code that has been executed after the deployment of a virtual machine:

```
    "outputs": {
      "customScriptOutput": {
        "type": "string",
        "value":
    "[reference('firstCustomScriptExtension').instanceView.substatuses[0].messa
    ge]"
      }
    }
```

The output from this execution is shown in the following screenshot:

```
Outputs          :
                  Name              Type                    Value
                  customScriptOutput  String                VERBOSE: Installation started... \n\nSuccess Restart Needed Exit Code      Feature Result
                  \n-              ---------                -------------                    \nTrue    No            NoChangeNeeded {}
                          \nVERBOSE: Installation succeeded.\n\n
```

Using CustomScriptExtension with Linux virtual machines

So far, we have looked at using Custom Script Extensions on Windows virtual machines, but it is also possible to use this resource for customizing Linux virtual machines. However, instead of a PowerShell script, we should use bash scripts.

Readers should note that with PowerShell Core 6.0, it is also possible to execute PowerShell scripts on a Linux operating system.

As we get started, we need a simple bash script that can be used without a Custom Script Extension.

The script we've chosen does nothing special; it simply outputs the supplied parameters and generates a random number. This script is stored with a .sh file extension. The code for the following bash script is available in the first.sh file in the accompanying chapter code:

```bash
#!/bin/bash
var="FOOsball"
echo $var
echo "Ritesh Modi"
echo $1
echo $2
date +"%T"
echo $RANDOM
$RANDOM
```

The extension resource configuration is shown in the following example. The code for this example is available in the Linux-CSA.json file in the accompanying chapter code:

```
{
    "apiVersion": "2015-06-15",
    "type": "Microsoft.Compute/virtualMachines/extensions",
    "name": "[concat(variables('vmName'), '/', 'linuxscripts')]",
    "location": "[resourceGroup().location]",
    "dependsOn": [
        "[concat('Microsoft.Compute/virtualMachines/', variables('vmName'))]"
    ],
    "tags": {
        "displayName": "config-app"
    },
    "properties": {
        "publisher": "Microsoft.OSTCExtensions",
        "type": "CustomScriptForLinux",
        "typeHandlerVersion": "1.2",
        "autoUpgradeMinorVersion": true,
        "settings": {
            "fileUris": [
"https://allarmfiles.blob.core.windows.net/armfiles/first.sh"
            ],
            "commandToExecute": "[concat('sh first.sh ','argument1 ','argument2 ', 'argument 3 ')]"
        }
    }
}
```

IaaS Solutions Using Templates

The extension type for a Linux virtual machine is `CustomScriptForLinux` and its publisher name is `Microsoft.OSTCExtensions`, which is similar to its Windows counterpart. Here, a bash file is supplied and executed via arguments.

Desired State Configuration

Desired State Configuration (DSC) is a relatively new configuration management offering from Microsoft. It is not an end product but rather a platform that you can use to build your own custom configuration management system. It is similar to tools already available like Ansible, Chef, and Puppet. DSC is a lightweight configuration management platform that can run on-premises as well as in the cloud.

We will not go into what DSC is and how it works in detail in this chapter. There is ample text available to access on the internet and in existing literature. Instead, in this section, we will look at how to apply DSC to virtual machines using extensions.

Note that a target virtual machine must have internet and the appropriate network security group rules enabled in order to download the DSC locally. It is also important to remember that there can be only one desired state extension per virtual machine. The extensions cannot be run on the same virtual machine either serially or in parallel.

Let's understand the DSC extension with the help of the following example:

```
{
    "type": "extensions",
    "apiVersion": "2015-06-15",
    "name": "Microsoft.Powershell.DSC",
    "location": "[resourceGroup().location]",
    "dependsOn": [
"[resourceId('Microsoft.Compute/virtualMachines',variables('vmName'))]"
    ],
    "properties": {
      "publisher": "Microsoft.Powershell",
      "type": "DSC",
      "typeHandlerVersion": "2.9",
      "autoUpgradeMinorVersion": true,
      "settings": {
        "Configuration": {
          "url":
"https://allarmfiles.blob.core.windows.net/dscfiles/psdsc.ps1.zip",
          "script": "psdsc.ps1",
          "function": "Main"
        }
    }
```

```
        }
    }
```

As you can see, DSC is similar to a Custom Script Extension, except in its settings. Here, the `type` is `DSC` and the `publisher` is `Microsoft.Powershell`. The settings have three properties.

`URL` refers to the location of the ZIP file containing the configuration, the `script` property refers to the PowerShell script file that should be executed, and the `function` property refers to the name of the configuration that should be executed.

Let's now map these properties to a DSC configuration, as shown in the following snippet. The code for this PowerShell script is available in the `psdsc.ps1` file in the accompanying chapter code:

```
Configuration Main
{
    Import-DscResource -ModuleName PSDesiredStateConfiguration
    node localhost
    {
        WindowsFeature iis
        {
            Name = "Web-Server"
            Ensure = "present"
        }
    }
}
```

As you can see in the previous code, the name of the configuration is `Main` and the name of the PowerShell script containing this configuration is `psdsc.ps1`, which is listed in the `script` property. We should also add that when this file is uploaded to a storage account, it is uploaded as a ZIP file.

The DSC configuration is authored in PowerShell ISE and then uploaded to an Azure storage account. The PowerShell command required to upload a ZIP file from DSC is as follows:

```
Publish-AzureRmVMDscConfiguration -ResourceGroupName armfiles -
ConfigurationPath "C:\Users\rites\psdsc.ps1" `
-ContainerName templates -StorageAccountName armtfiles -Force -Verbose
```

`Publish-AzureRmVMDscConfiguration` will take the configuration provided through the `ConfigurationPath` parameter and generate a ZIP file containing the original PowerShell script file before uploading it to an Azure storage account container.

[135]

IaaS Solutions Using Templates

The output of this command is shown in the following screenshot:

```
PS C:\WINDOWS\system32>>>>> Publish-AzureRmVMDscConfiguration -ResourceGroupName armfiles -ConfigurationPath "C:\Users\rites\
VERBOSE: Temp folder 'C:\Users\rites\AppData\Local\Temp\a92b0f86-116c-4f8d-927b-8c84cf0c1614' created.
VERBOSE: Copy 'C:\users\rites\Desktop\A - Chapter5 - Copy\psdsc.ps1' to 'C:\Users\rites\AppData\Local\Temp\a92b0f86-116c-4f8d
VERBOSE: Parsing configuration script: C:\Users\rites\Desktop\A - Chapter5 - Copy\psdsc.ps1
VERBOSE: List of required modules: [].
VERBOSE: Temp folder 'C:\Users\rites\AppData\Local\Temp\dc7226e9-4fd1-4479-acdc-61f80ba087f2' created.
VERBOSE: Performing the operation "Upload 'C:\Users\rites\AppData\Local\Temp\dc7226e9-4fd1-4479-acdc-61f80ba087f2\psdsc.ps1.z
tes/psdsc.ps1.zip'".
VERBOSE: Configuration published to https://armfiles.blob.core.windows.net/templates/psdsc.ps1.zip
https://armfiles.blob.core.windows.net/templates/psdsc.ps1.zip
VERBOSE: Deleted 'C:\Users\rites\AppData\Local\Temp\dc7226e9-4fd1-4479-acdc-61f80ba087f2\psdsc.ps1.zip'
VERBOSE: Deleted 'C:\Users\rites\AppData\Local\Temp\a92b0f86-116c-4f8d-927b-8c84cf0c1614'
VERBOSE: Deleted 'C:\Users\rites\AppData\Local\Temp\dc7226e9-4fd1-4479-acdc-61f80ba087f2'
```

Let's now take a look at the `parameter` section of the template in our DSC configuration, as follows:

```
"storageAccountName": {
    "type": "string"
},
"containerName": {
    "type": "string"
},
"zipfileName": {
    "type": "string"
},
"fileName": {
    "type": "string"
}
```

As you can see, four `parameters` specific to DSC are accepted. They are used to accept the storage account domain name, the container name within the storage account, the ZIP file containing the configuration, and the PowerShell script file name.

The resource configuration for DSC is shown in the following snippet. The code for this example is available in the `Dsc-Basic.json` file in the accompanying chapter code:

```
{
    "type": "extensions",
    "apiVersion": "2015-06-15",
    "name": "Microsoft.Powershell.DSC",
    "location": "[resourceGroup().location]",
    "dependsOn": [
        "[resourceId('Microsoft.Compute/virtualMachines',variables('vmName'))]"
    ],
    "properties": {
        "publisher": "Microsoft.Powershell",
        "type": "DSC",
        "typeHandlerVersion": "2.9",
        "autoUpgradeMinorVersion": true,
```

```
            "settings": {
              "Configuration": {
                "url":
"[concat(parameters('storageAccountName'),'/',parameters('containerName'),'
/',parameters('zipfileName'))]",
                "script": "[parameters('fileName')]",
                "function": "Main"
              }
            }
          }
        }
```

This is a nested configuration within a virtual machine's resources section. The parameters seen in the preceding example are used to provide value to existing configuration settings.

Now it's time to execute the template using PowerShell, as follows:

```
New-AzureRmResourceGroupDeployment -Name "csa01" -ResourceGroupName test01
-Mode Incremental -TemplateFile
"c:\users\rites\source\repos\AzureResourceGroup19\Dsc-Basic.json" -
adminUsername "superadmin" -adminPassword $(ConvertTo-SecureString -String
Pa55w0rdPa55w0rd -AsPlainText -Force) -dnsNameForPublicIP armtemplateunique
-storageAccountName "https://armtfiles.blob.core.windows.net" -
containerName templates -zipfileName psdsc.ps1.zip -fileName psdsc.ps1 -
Verbose
```

As you can see, all of the parameters expected by the ARM template are provided while the deployment of the template is executed.

Using configuration data

Configuration data in DSC helps to define configuration settings and values across its different environments. This data acts in a similar way to the Azure ARM template parameters file.

Instead of hardcoding values within DSC configurations, the values can be stored in an external configuration and reused across multiple environments. You can find more information about configuration data in Microsoft documents.

Let's now look at configuration data at work in a DSC configuration and deploy it on an Azure virtual machine using an ARM template.

IaaS Solutions Using Templates

The PowerShell DSC configuration is shown in the following snippet. The code for this PowerShell script is available in the `psdsc-configdata.ps1` file in the accompanying chapter code:

```
Configuration Main

{
    [CmdletBinding()]
    Param (
    [string]$serviceName
    )
    Import-DscResource -ModuleName PSDesiredStateConfiguration
    node $AllNodes.Where{$_.Role -eq "WebServer"}.Nodename
    {
        WindowsFeature iis
        {
            Name = $serviceName
            Ensure = $AllNodes.Where{$_.Role -eq "WebServer"}.IsPresent
        }
    }
}
```

Readers should pay special attention to the syntax used to read the configuration data.

The configuration data used for DSC configuration is illustrated in the following snippet. The code for this PowerShell script is available in the `configdata.psd1` file in the accompanying chapter code:

```
# Configuration Data for AD
@{
    AllNodes = @(
        @{
            NodeName="*"
            RetryCount = 20
            RetryIntervalSec = 30
            PSDscAllowPlainTextPassword=$true
            PSDscAllowDomainUser = $true
        },
        @{
            Nodename = "localhost"
            Role = "WebServer"
            IsPresent = "present"
        }
    )
}
```

As you can see, the configuration should be stored in a `.ps1` file extension, while configuration data should be stored in a `psd1` extension. Both of these files can be stored on the file system and later supplied to the `Publish-AzureRmVMDSCConfiguration` cmdlet.

Uploading DSC configuration has two steps: first, we need to add the DSC configuration file before adding the configuration data file. To upload the DSC configuration, execute the following PowerShell command:

```
Publish-AzureRmVMDscConfiguration -ResourceGroupName armfiles -
ConfigurationPath "C:\Users\rites\psdsc-configdata.ps1" -ContainerName
templates -StorageAccountName armtfiles -ConfigurationDataPath
"C:\Users\rites\configdata.psd1" -Force -Verbose
```

The difference between this command and others we've looked at previously is the addition of the `ConfigurationDataPath` argument, which points to the newly-created `PSD1` file.

The `PSD1` file can be uploaded separately using `Set-AzureStorageBlobcontent`, or it can be uploaded manually to an Azure storage account.

The template for using DSC artifacts is shown in the following snippet. The code for this example is available in the `DSC-ConfigData.json` file in the accompanying chapter code:

```json
{
    "type": "extensions",
    "apiVersion": "2015-06-15",
    "name": "Microsoft.Powershell.DSC",
    "location": "[resourceGroup().location]",
    "dependsOn": [
"[resourceId('Microsoft.Compute/virtualMachines',variables('vmName'))]"
    ],
    "properties": {
      "publisher": "Microsoft.Powershell",
      "type": "DSC",
      "typeHandlerVersion": "2.9",
      "autoUpgradeMinorVersion": true,
      "settings": {
        "Configuration": {
          "url":
"https://armtfiles.blob.core.windows.net/templates/psdsc-configdata.ps1.zip
",
          "script": "psdsc-configdata.ps1",
          "function": "Main"
        },
        "configurationArguments": {
          "serviceName": "XPS-Viewer"
        },
        "configurationData": {
```

```
                    "url":
"https://armtfiles.blob.core.windows.net/templates/configdata.psd1"
                    }
                }
            }
        }
```

The configuration settings here are similar to previous examples. However, there are two additional settings to note, as follows:

- The `ConfigurationArguments` setting is used to supply parameters to DSC configuration. Please note that DSC configuration in this example expects a parameter, `serviceName`, which should be supplied by the ARM template. The value supplied here is `XPS-Viewer`.
- The `ConfigurationData` setting is used to provide the location of configuration data to an extension such that it can extract the values and provide them to DSC configuration running within a virtual machine during ARM template deployment.

Summary

This chapter focused extensively on extension resources. Extension resources help to configure virtual machines after they are deployed, and there are multiple types available. In this chapter, we investigated `customscriptextension` and DSC extension, which can both be executed against virtual machines. Extensions help to configure the inside of a virtual machine.

In the next chapter, we will look at unit testing ARM templates using Pester.

6
Unit Testing ARM Templates

So far, we have been authoring and provisioning resources, using the ARM template. Provisioning resources using ARM templates is the preferred mechanism and enables infrastructure-as-code practices. As we write code to provision our infrastructure, it is important to test the deployment and the resources. These tests should be done on individual resources as well as collectively, to ensure that they are working together appropriately.

Although writing unit tests is not a new concept, it is a new paradigm to unit test infrastructure, environments, and deployments. In this chapter, we will investigate ways to unit test the ARM template deployments and environments.

We will specifically cover the following:

- Unit testing as a concept
- Unit testing ARM templates
- Retrieving outputs from ARM templates
- Pester as a unit testing tool
- Setting up the test harness

Unit testing

Unit testing refers to the process of testing each piece of code in isolation. Typically, unit tests are written for application code, such as for web applications, middleware services, and desktop applications. With cloud deployments gaining popularity, it is needed to test the resources provisioned using ARM templates, to validate their configurations.

The process of unit testing is quite simple. Let's understand this process using an example: So, let's assume we want to unit test a function that simply adds together two numbers. The function has a single line of code that adds two numbers that are supplied as parameters to the function. Such a unit testing scenario's function would be like the following:

- Using two positive numbers and the resulting actual added value should match the expected value, and it should be a positive number greater than both the numbers
- Using two negative numbers, and the resulting actual addition should again match the expected value, and it should be a negative number bigger than both the numbers
- Using just one of the numbers should result in an exception
- Not sending any value should again result in an exception
- Sending a value of a type other than a number should result in an exception

And there could be more—however, I'm sure you've got the idea!

You have probably noticed that the process of unit testing involves comparing two values. The first value is the value that comes from the execution of the function, and the other value is the expected value. This means that during unit testing, we should know the expected value from the execution of each unit test. The actual and expected values are compared and based on the result, and either the unit test is flagged as passed or failed.

Unit testing can be executed by comparing values using a conditional statement of equality, greater than, less than, not equal, and even exceptions.

Unit testing ARM templates

In the case of ARM templates, we define and declare resources using JSON notation. There is no value in testing this JSON file consisting of parameters and resources by parsing it. These templates do not generate any assemblies that can be used for executing unit tests against them. These templates can only be deployed, and so the only way to unit test resources in an ARM template is to unit test them after the deployment of the ARM template.

For the purposes of this chapter, we will use the next template for unit testing. This template is available with this chapter's accompanied code file named `chapter-6 - listing1.txt`. This template creates five resources:

- Azure Storage account
- Azure Virtual Network
- Azure public IP address
- Azure network interface card
- Azure Virtual Machine

The `parameters` defined for this template are shown next:

```
      "parameters": {
        "adminUsername": {
          "type": "string",
          "metadata": {
            "description": "Username for the Virtual Machine."
          }
        },
        "adminPassword": {
          "type": "securestring",
          "metadata": {
            "description": "Password for the Virtual Machine."
          }
        },
        "dnsLabelPrefix": {
          "type": "string",
          "metadata": {
            "description": "Unique DNS Name for the Public IP used to access
   the Virtual Machine."
          }
        },
        "windowsOSVersion": {
          "type": "string",
          "defaultValue": "2016-Datacenter",
          "allowedValues": [
            "2016-Datacenter-with-Containers",
            "2016-Datacenter"
          ],
          "metadata": {
            "description": "The Windows version for the VM."
          }
        },
        "location": {
          "type": "string",
          "defaultValue": "[resourceGroup().location]",
```

```
      "metadata": {
        "description": "Location for all resources."
      }
    }
  },
```

The `variables` for this template are shown next:

```
      "storageAccountName": "[concat(uniquestring(resourceGroup().id),
'sawinvm')]",
      "imagePublisher": "MicrosoftWindowsServer",
      "imageOffer": "WindowsServer",
      "nicName": "myVMNic",
      "addressPrefix": "10.0.0.0/16",
      "subnetName": "Subnet",
      "subnetPrefix": "10.0.0.0/24",
      "publicIPAddressName": "myPublicIP",
      "OSDiskName": "osdiskforwindowssimple",
      "vhdStorageContainerName": "vhds",
      "vmName": "MyWindowsVM",
      "vmSize": "Standard_A2",
      "virtualNetworkName": "MyVNET",
      "subnetRef": "[resourceId('Microsoft.Network/virtualNetworks/subnets',
variables('virtualNetworkName'), variables('subnetName'))]"
```

The storage account resource configuration is shown next:

```
    {
      "type": "Microsoft.Storage/storageAccounts",
      "name": "[variables('storageAccountName')]",
      "apiVersion": "2016-01-01",
      "location": "[parameters('location')]",
      "sku": {
        "name": "Standard_LRS"
      },
      "kind": "Storage",
      "properties": {}
    }
```

The public IP address resource configuration is shown next. Possible values for the IP allocation method are `Dynamic` and `Static`. The `domainNameLabel` property value should be a unique value globally within Azure. It becomes part of the DNS name:

```
    {
      "apiVersion": "2016-03-30",
      "type": "Microsoft.Network/publicIPAddresses",
      "name": "[variables('publicIPAddressName')]",
      "location": "[parameters('location')]",
```

```
    "properties": {
      "publicIPAllocationMethod": "Dynamic",
      "dnsSettings": {
        "domainNameLabel": "[parameters('dnsLabelPrefix')]"
      }
    }
},
```

The virtual network resource configuration is shown next. It has just one subnet, although it is possible to create more subnets:

```
{
    "apiVersion": "2016-03-30",
    "type": "Microsoft.Network/virtualNetworks",
    "name": "[variables('virtualNetworkName')]",
    "location": "[parameters('location')]",
    "properties": {
      "addressSpace": {
        "addressPrefixes": [
          "[variables('addressPrefix')]"
        ]
      },
      "subnets": [
        {
          "name": "[variables('subnetName')]",
          "properties": {
            "addressPrefix": "[variables('subnetPrefix')]"
          }
        }
      ]
    }
}
```

There are no dependencies between the resource until now. The next resource configuration is the **Network Interface Card** (**NIC**), and it has dependency on both the public IP address and the virtual network. The private IP address allocated to it on the virtual network is `Dynamic`, meaning that the virtual network will assign the next available IP address:

```
{
    "apiVersion": "2016-03-30",
    "type": "Microsoft.Network/networkInterfaces",
    "name": "[variables('nicName')]",
    "location": "[parameters('location')]",
    "dependsOn": [
      "[resourceId('Microsoft.Network/publicIPAddresses/', variables('publicIPAddressName'))]",
```

Unit Testing ARM Templates

```
        "[resourceId('Microsoft.Network/virtualNetworks/',
variables('virtualNetworkName'))]"
      ],
      "properties": {
        "ipConfigurations": [
          {
            "name": "ipconfig1",
            "properties": {
              "privateIPAllocationMethod": "Dynamic",
              "publicIPAddress": {
                "id":
"[resourceId('Microsoft.Network/publicIPAddresses',variables('publicIPAddressName'))]"
              },
              "subnet": {
                "id": "[variables('subnetRef')]"
              }
            }
          }
        ]
      }
    }
```

By now, we have all the needed resources for creating a virtual machine. The virtual machine will be dependent on the availability of the storage account for storing its OS and data disks, and on the NIC, for communicating to the virtual network and the outside world.

The virtual machine configuration is shown next:

```
    {
      "apiVersion": "2015-06-15",
      "type": "Microsoft.Compute/virtualMachines",
      "name": "[variables('vmName')]",
      "location": "[resourceGroup().location]",
      "tags": {
        "displayName": "VirtualMachine"
      },
      "dependsOn": [
        "[concat('Microsoft.Storage/storageAccounts/',
variables('storageAccountName'))]",
        "[concat('Microsoft.Network/networkInterfaces/',
variables('nicName'))]"
      ],
      "properties": {
        "hardwareProfile": {
          "vmSize": "[variables('vmSize')]"
        },
```

```
      "osProfile": {
        "computerName": "[variables('vmName')]",
        "adminUsername": "[parameters('adminUsername')]",
        "adminPassword": "[parameters('adminPassword')]"
      },
      "storageProfile": {
        "imageReference": {
          "publisher": "[variables('imagePublisher')]",
          "offer": "[variables('imageOffer')]",
          "sku": "[parameters('windowsOSVersion')]",
          "version": "latest"
        },
        "osDisk": {
          "name": "osdisk",
          "vhd": {
            "uri": "[concat('https://', variables('storageAccountName'), '.blob.core.windows.net/', variables('vhdStorageContainerName'), '/', variables('OSDiskName'), '.vhd')]"
          },
          "caching": "ReadWrite",
          "createOption": "FromImage"
        }
      },
      "networkProfile": {
        "networkInterfaces": [
          {
            "id": "[resourceId('Microsoft.Network/networkInterfaces', variables('nicName'))]"
          }
        ]
      }
    }
  }
```

And, finally, the `outputs` section returns the values related to all five resources:

```
"outputs": {
  "storageAccount": {
    "type": "object",
    "value": "[reference(variables('storageAccountName'))]"
  },
  "publicIPAddressName": {
    "type": "object",
    "value": "[reference(variables('publicIPAddressName'))]"
  },
  "virtualNetworkName": {
    "type": "object",
    "value": "[reference(variables('virtualNetworkName'))]"
```

```
        },
        "nicName": {
          "type": "object",
          "value": "[reference(variables('nicName'))]"
        },
        "vmName": {
          "type": "object",
          "value": "[reference(variables('vmName'))]"
        }
    }
}
```

There is nothing unique in this template, and it is similar to the other templates we have seen so far, but with one difference. In this template, you have probably noticed that the `outputs` section of the template `outputs` the entire resource output for all the resources. There is one corresponding output section for each resource declared within the template. It is this output we are interested in for unit testing ARM templates.

The template can be deployed using PowerShell, as shown next:

```
New-AzureRmResourceGroupDeployment -Name "csa01" -ResourceGroupName test01
-Mode Incremental -TemplateFile
"C:\Users\rites\Desktop\Chapter7\templateforUnitTests.json" -adminUsername
"superadmin" -adminPassword $(ConvertTo-SecureString -String
Pa55w0rdPa55w0rd -AsPlainText -Force) -dnsLabelPrefix armtemplateunique -
Verbose
```

The most important element in this command is the name of the deployment. Using this name, it is possible to pull out the `outputs` from the ARM template execution at a later point of time, using PowerShell.

Retrieving outputs from ARM templates

Azure PowerShell provides the cmdlet `Get-AzureRmResourceGroupDeployment` and accepts the name of the deployment, along with name of the resource group. Using this cmdlet, we can retrieve the output of any past deployment. It is important to know the name of the deployment and the resource group name before this cmdlet can be used. It expects these two parameters for returning outputs of the past deployment.

Let's execute this command to retrieve the deployment outputs, using the same name used during the deployment of an ARM template. Notice that `test01` was the resource group to which we deployed the previous ARM template and the name of the deployment was `csa01`:

```
Get-AzureRmResourceGroupDeployment -ResourceGroupName test01 -Name csa01 -Verbose
```

The output from this command is quite verbose, and it is not shown completely, for the sake of brevity. However, a small snapshot is shown in the following screenshot. The return from this command contains generated outputs of the storage account, public IP address, and the virtual network from past deployment:

```
Outputs                :
                         Name                  Type                             Value
                         ====================  ===============================  ==========
                         storageAccount        Object                           {
                           "encryption": {
                             "services": {
                               "blob": {
                                 "enabled": true,
                                 "lastEnabledTime": "2018-09-08T06:08:09.9525584Z"
                               }
                             },
                             "keySource": "Microsoft.Storage"
                           },
                           "provisioningState": "Succeeded",
                           "creationTime": "2018-09-08T06:08:09.7964977Z",
                           "primaryEndpoints": {
                             "blob": "https://3rs257t55vn4asawinvm.blob.core.windows.net/",
                             "queue": "https://3rs257t55vn4asawinvm.queue.core.windows.net/",
                             "table": "https://3rs257t55vn4asawinvm.table.core.windows.net/",
                             "file": "https://3rs257t55vn4asawinvm.file.core.windows.net/"
                           },
                           "primaryLocation": "westeurope",
                           "statusOfPrimary": "available"
                         }
                         publicIPAddressName   Object                           {
                           "provisioningState": "Succeeded",
                           "resourceGuid": "65027abf-f957-4fae-82ee-138e4e7963eb",
                           "publicIPAddressVersion": "IPv4",
                           "publicIPAllocationMethod": "Dynamic",
                           "idleTimeoutInMinutes": 4,
                           "dnsSettings": {
                             "domainNameLabel": "armtemplateunique",
                             "fqdn": "armtemplateunique.westeurope.cloudapp.azure.com"
                           }
                         }
                         virtualNetworkName    Object                           {
                           "provisioningState": "Succeeded",
                           "resourceGuid": "60c2f659-b0bd-4507-a1b6-257929b5d154",
                           "addressSpace": {
                             "addressPrefixes": [
                               "10.0.0.0/16"
```

Using Pester

Pester is used to test PowerShell's scripts and functions. It can be used for the unit testing of templates as well.

Pester provides the necessary infrastructure to ease the process of writing unit tests in PowerShell. It provides facilities to write test cases, execute, and report back results. It is an open source utility available as a PowerShell module. By default, it is available in Windows Server 2016 and Windows 10. For other operating systems, it can be installed using the following:

```
Install-Module cmdlet
```

Writing unit tests using Pester is quite simple. It provides functions for declaring tests, as well as assertions. Assertions refer to the process of comparing and validating two variables. A simple Pester script in PowerShell is shown next. In this example, unit tests are written against a simple function that adds two numbers together.

Pester provides the `Describe` function for defining a test suite. It contains multiple test cases. It takes a string value to describe the test suite. The `BeforeAll` function is the first function executed and typically used for initializing the test suite. It is here that variables are initialized and other conditions prepared as a starting position before individual unit tests are executed.

The actual tests are written using the `It` function. It takes a name and a script. The actual comparison between actual and expected values happens within this script. There are multiple assertions provided by Pester, and one of them is `Should Be`, which does an equality comparison. There are other *Assertions* defined here: `https://github.com/pester/Pester/tree/master/Functions/Assertions`.

The `Context` function is a placeholder function for distinguishing between different scenarios within the same test suite. There are two contexts in the next example—one of them contains a single test case and the other contains two test cases.

These tests can be executed using the `invoke-pester` cmdlet and passing the script as its parameter. They can also be executed on the PowerShell ISE Window directly:

```
function AddTwoNumbers([int] $a, [int] $b) {
    return $a + $b
}
 $firstValue, $secondValue
 Describe "Addition Validation Tests" {
   BeforeAll {
        $firstValue = 10
```

```
            $secondValue = 20;
        }
    Context "using Global variables" {
            It "Adding two positive numbers" {
                AddTwoNumbers -a $firstValue -b $secondValue | Should Be 30
            }
        }
    Context "Using Local Variables" {
            It "Adding two positive numbers" {
            $firstValue = 100
            $secondValue = 200
                AddTwoNumbers -a $firstValue -b $secondValue | Should Be 300
            }
            It "Adding two negative numbers" {
                $firstValue = -100
                $secondValue=-200
                AddTwoNumbers -a $firstValue -b $secondValue | Should Be -300
            }
        }
    }
}
```

Setting up the test harness

To test resources deployed using the ARM template, it is important that the template deployment generates the necessary outputs that can be read later for testing purposes. Since this activity has already been taken care of, it's time to read the outputs. The outputs from the ARM template can be read using `Get-AzureRmResouceGroupDeployment` and passing the name of the deployment, along with the resource group's name. The returned output from this cmdlet can be used to retrieve the outputs individually. This code should be placed within the `BeforeAll` function of Pester so that it can be executed before any of the test cases are executed.

The code shown next gets all the outputs for each resource and stores them into individual variables. Notice the name used to get the values. It is the same as that used in the *output* section of the ARM template:

```
    BeforeAll {
$deployment =  (Get-AzureRmResourceGroupDeployment -ResourceGroupName
$deploymentName   -Name $deploymentName)
$storage = $deployment.Outputs.storageaccount.Value
$publicIP = $deployment.Outputs.publicIPAddressName.Value
$nic = $deployment.Outputs.nicName.Value
```

```
$virtualNetwork = $deployment.Outputs.virtualNetworkName.Value
$virtualMachine = $deployment.Outputs.vmName.Value
    }
```

Unit testing of a storage account

There can be many unit tests that can be written for each resource. I am providing some sample unit tests that can be executed for each of five resources we have in the template. In the script shown next for testing a deployed storage account, test cases related to the successful provisioning of the storage account, its available state, and its location are validated.

You should note that the expected value is already known and should be used to check against the actual value obtained from deployment. This code file is available with the accompanied code file, `chapter-6 - listing6.txt`:

```
Context "Storage from template deployment" {
    It "The storage account has been provisioned successfully"
{
        [string]$storage.provisioningState | Should Be "Succeeded"
    }

    It "The storage account is in available state" {
        [string]$storage.statusOfPrimary | Should Be "available"
    }

    It "The storage account location is West Europe" {
        [string]$storage.primaryLocation | Should Be "westeurope"
    }
}
```

Unit testing a public IP address

The next script is for testing a deployed public IP address. The test cases are for validating a successful deployment and allocation method—dynamic or static. This code file is available with the accompanied code file, `chapter-6 - listing7.txt`:

```
Context "Public IP address from template deployment" {
    It "The public IP address resource Have been deployed successfully" {
        [string]$publicIP.provisioningState | Should Be "Succeeded"
    }
    It "The Public IP address is allocation dynamic IP address" {
```

```
                    [string]$publicIP.publicIPAllocationMethod | Should Be
"Dynamic"
            }
        }
```

Unit testing virtual networks

Testing a virtual network involves validating successful deployment, the virtual network address range, the subnet address range, the number of subnets, and whether the subnets have been provisioned successfully. The same has been shown in the next script example. This code file is available with the accompanied code file, `chapter-6 - listing8.txt`:

```
        Context "virtual network from template deployment" {
            It "The virtual network has been provisioned successfully" {
                [string]$virtualNetwork.provisioningState | Should Be
"Succeeded"
            }
            It "The address range for virtual network is "10.0.0.0/16" {
                [string]$virtualNetwork.addressSpace.addressPrefixes |
Should Be "10.0.0.0/16"
            }
            It "The count of subnets in virtual network is 1" {
                [int]$virtualNetwork.subnets.Count | Should Be 1
            }
            It "The IP address range for subnet is "10.0.0.0/24"{
                [string]$virtualNetwork.subnets[0].properties.addressPrefix |
Should Be "10.0.0.0/24"
            }
            It "The subnet has been provisioned successfully" {
[string]$virtualNetwork.subnets[0].properties.provisioningState   | Should
Be "Succeeded"
            }
        }
```

Unit testing an NIC

Testing an NIC involves validating whether it was successfully created, determining whether it is the primary NIC, whether IP forwarding is enabled, whether the IP allocation method matches the provided configuration and the associated subnet on the virtual network and the related IP address. You should pay attention to the syntax used to get the public IP address reference in test cases, using the `Get-AzureRmResource` cmdlet.

Unit Testing ARM Templates

The entire code has been broken into two code listings for easy reading. The entire code listing is available within the `chapter-6 - listing9.txt` file with the chapter-accompanied code. The first part of it checks for `provisioningState`, primary NIC, status of IP forwarding, status, and primary NIC IP configuration:

```
Context "Network Interface from template deployment" {
    It "The NIC Have been provisioned successfully" {
            [string]$nic.provisioningState | Should Be "Succeeded"
        }

    It "Is primary NIC" {
            [string]$nic.primary | Should Be true
        }

    It "IP forwarding is disabled on NIC" {
            [int]$nic.enableIPForwarding | Should Be 0
        }

    It "The NIC IP configuration was provisioned successfully" {
[string]$nic.ipConfigurations[0].properties.provisioningState | Should Be "Succeeded"
        }

    It "The NIC is the primary Nic" {
                [string]$nic.ipConfigurations[0].properties.primary | Should Be true
        }
```

The second part of the code checks for the IP allocation method. It should match the same value that was used in the ARM template while provisioning the NIC. We had used a `Dynamic` value for the IP allocation method, and the same check is made here. We also check whether the NIC is associated with the provided subnet on the virtual network and also is associated with a valid public IP address resource:

```
It "The IP allocation method used for NIC is dynamic" {
    [string]$nic.ipConfigurations[0].properties.privateIPAllocationMethod | Should Be "Dynamic"
  }

It "The NIC is associated to appropriate subnet" {
     [string]$nic.ipConfigurations[0].properties.subnet.id  | should be $([string]$virtualNetwork.subnets[0].id)
  }

It "NIC is referencing the appropriate public IP resource" {
       [string]$nic.ipConfigurations[0].properties.publicIPAddress.id  |
```

```
    should be  $(Get-AzureRmResource -ResourceId
$([string]$nic.ipConfigurations[0].properties.publicIPAddress.id)).Resource
id
}
```

Unit testing a virtual machine

Testing a virtual machine involves validating successful deployment, the size of the virtual machine, image details such as SKU, publisher, and offer; the attached NIC; the availability and installation of agents; switched-on automated updates; the type of operating system—Linux or Windows; details about the OS disk; disk caching; and more. This code file is available with the accompanied code file, `chapter-6 - listing10.txt`.

The entire code has been broken into two code-listings, for easy reading. The first part of it checks for `provisioningState`, primary NIC, the status of IP forwarding, status, and the primary NIC IP configuration:

```
Context "Virtual Machine from template deployment" {
    It "The virtual machine is provisioned successfully" {
        [string]$virtualMachine.provisioningState | Should Be "Succeeded"
    }

    It "The size of virtual machine is $($deployment.Parameters.virtualMachineSize.Value)" {
        [string]$virtualMachine.hardwareProfile.vmSize | Should Be "Standard_A2"
    }
    It "The virtual machine is attached to appropriate NIC" {
        [string]$virtualMachine.networkProfile.networkInterfaces[0].id | Should Be $(Get-                AzureRmResource -ResourceId
$([string]$virtualMachine.networkProfile.networkInterfaces[0].id)).Resource
id
    }
    It "The virtual machine is enabled for automatic update" {
[bool]$virtualMachine.osProfile.windowsConfiguration.enableAutomaticUpdates
| Should Be true
    }
    It "VM agent is provisioned within virtual machine" {
[bool]$virtualMachine.osProfile.windowsConfiguration.provisionVMAgent |
Should Be true
    }
    It "The SKU of virtual machine image is $($deployment.Parameters.imageReferenceSku.Value)" {
        [string]$virtualMachine.storageProfile.imageReference.sku | Should Be "2016-Datacenter"
```

Unit Testing ARM Templates

```
            }
        It "The offer of virtual machine image is
$($deployment.Parameters.imageReferenceOffer.Value)" {
            [string]$virtualMachine.storageProfile.imageReference.offer   |
Should Be "WindowsServer"
        }
```

The second part of the code checks for the image publisher, type of operating system, size of OS disk, and other properties:

```
            It "The publisher of virtual machine image is
$($deployment.Parameters.imageReferencePublisher.Value)" {
    [string]$virtualMachine.storageProfile.imageReference.publisher   | Should
Be "MicrosoftWindowsServer"
        }
        It "The virtual machine is based on Windows operating system" {
            [string]$virtualMachine.storageProfile.osDisk.osType |
Should Be "Windows"
        }
        It "The virtual machine is creating using an Image" {
            [string]$virtualMachine.storageProfile.osDisk.createOption
| Should Be "FromImage"
        }
        It "The size of virtual machine os disk is 127 GB" {
            [int]$virtualMachine.storageProfile.osDisk.diskSizeGB   |
Should Be 127
        }
        It "The caching is ReadWrite for virtual machine os disk" {
            [string]$virtualMachine.storageProfile.osDisk.caching   |
Should Be "ReadWrite"
        }
    }
```

The complete unit test script

The entire unit testing code is available as a `chapter-6 - listing11.txt` file with the accompanied chapter code. Note that this script takes two parameters—the name of the deployment and the name of the resource group. These parameters are used to retrieve the outputs values, using the PowerShell `Get-AzureRmResourceGroupDeployment` cmdlet.

The command to execute the entire unit testing script is shown next. The `invoke-pester` command is used to run the unit tests, and it accepts the script parameter. This parameter accepts a hash table consisting of the path of the script file and any arguments accepted by the script file. The arguments are supplied as a hash table:

```
invoke-pester -Script @{path = "C:\Users\rites\Desktop\code File - ARM
book\chapter-6 - listing11.ps1
"; Parameters=@{deploymentName ='test1'; resourceGroupName = 'ARMPatterns'
} }
```

Executing the preceding script, either using `invoke-pester` or directly on PowerShell, will result in the following output:

```
Describing Validation Tests
   Context Storage from template deployment
     [+] The storage account has been provisioned successfully 4.6s
     [+] The storage account is in available state 24ms
     [+] The storage account location is West Europe 8ms
   Context virtual network from template deployment
     [+] The virtual network has been provisioned successfully 45ms
     [+] The address range for virtual network is  23ms
     [+] The count of subnets in virtual network is 1 19ms
     [+] The IP address range for subnet is  13ms
     [+] The subnet has been provisioned successfully 10ms
   Context Public IP address from template deployment
     [+] The public IP address resource Have been deployed successfully 44ms
     [+] The Public IP address is allocation dynamic IP address 18ms
   Context Network Interface from template deployment
     [+] The NIC Have been provisioned successfully 40ms
     [+] Is primary NIC 11ms
     [+] IP forwarding is disabled on NIC 20ms
     [+] TThe NIC IP configuration was provisioned successfully 16ms
     [+] The NIC is the primary Nic 21ms
     [+] The IP allocation method used for NIC is dynamic 15ms
     [+] The NIC is associated to appropriate subnet 16ms
     [+] NIC is referencing the appropriate public IP resource 15.53s
   Context Virtual Machine from template deployment
     [+] The virtual machine is provisioned successfully 35ms
     [+] The size of virtual machine is  14ms
     [+] The virtual machine is attached to appropriate NIC 5.79s
     [+] The virtual machine is enabled for automatic update 20ms
     [+] VM agent is provisioned within virtual machine 22ms
     [+] The SKU of virtual machine image is  15ms
     [+] The offer of virtual machine image is  15ms
     [+] The publisher of virtual machine image is  13ms
     [+] The virtual machine is based on Windows operating system 16ms
     [+] The virtual machine is creating using an Image 18ms
     [+] The size of virtual machine os disk is 127 GB 11ms
     [+] The caching is ReadWrite for virtual machine os disk 38ms
```

Summary

This chapter was about testing ARM templates. Maintaining the right quality of ARM templates is important, and it is a must to test ARM template deployments. Pester helps with providing the necessary infrastructure for testing ARM template deployments. It provides `Describe`, `It`, `Context`, and other necessary assertions to test ARM template deployment. One of the prerequisites for unit testing ARM templates is that the ARM templates should be authored in a way so that ARM outputs all the important information about resources. Reading this resource information and comparing it to the expected value helps to ascertain whether the deployment was successful and as expected, or whether there are deviations requiring another set of deployments, after the code has been corrected in ARM templates.

In the next chapter, we will understand how to write better maintainable, modular ARM templates.

7
Design Patterns

In previous chapters, you learned how to create simple as well as advanced ARM templates. In `Chapter 6`, *Unit Testing ARM Templates*, you learned about testing ARM templates as well. In this chapter, we are taking a step forward, and we are going to write ARM templates that are modular, reusable, and maintainable. The topics that will be covered in this chapter are as follows:

- Writing modular ARM templates
- Templates using Key Vault, for storing secrets
- Creating resource groups, using ARM templates
- Deploying resources in multiple resource groups simultaneously
- Using runtime values, from resources to configuring other resources
- Writing ARM templates and updating existing resources
- Writing ARM templates and deleting resources

This is an advanced topic, and you should have already read the previous chapters. If not, I would highly recommend reading them before getting started with this chapter.

Why use modular ARM templates?

Writing a single template consisting of Azure resources is quite common among developers. This is because it is easier and faster to author such ARM templates. However, this comes at a cost. These templates are not reusable, and it is difficult to maintain them. Consider a scenario where other projects might need to create some of the resources that are already in an existing ARM template. They cannot reuse this template before they modify it to suit their requirements. Alternatively, if the ARM templates are divided into multiple subtemplates, each consisting of a single or a few related resources, these sub-templates can be consumed directly by other projects.

Design Patterns

A single template is also difficult to maintain. Any changes in the ARM templates need to be verified across all the resources. Deploying a large template is more time-consuming than deploying subtemplates during the testing process. This improves the productivity of developers and testers.

In short, there are lots of advantages to using ARM templates writing in a modular fashion. So, the next question that arises is how to design modular ARM templates.

Single responsibility principle

Remember the good old single responsibility principle? The single responsibility principle states that any component or class should have a single responsibility; any changes to this responsibility should be the only reason for changing them. For example: A customer class should only manage a customer as its responsibility. It should not have any code related to orders or to the shopping cart. It means changes to the customer class should happen only when there is a change regarding customer behavior and rules, and not otherwise.

Known configuration/T-shirt sizing

If we apply the same principle to ARM templates, we can adopt the practice of writing ARM templates that have a single responsibility and a single reason to change.

This means ARM templates should have either of the following:

- **A single resource**: Changes to this resource should be the only reason to change the ARM template.
- **A group of related resources**: This represents either a functional grouping or a technical grouping. These ARM templates can further use nested or linked templates. These templates can also be called **intermediate templates**.

Eventually, there is a master or a main template that brings all the intermediate and single resource templates together to form a solution. This composition of ARM templates is also shown in the following diagram:

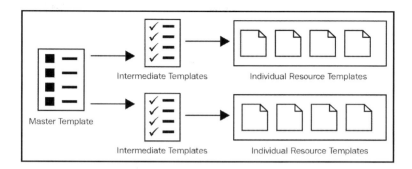

The **Master Template** is the initiation template, and it invokes other templates. The other templates could be shared templates. Shared templates are templates that can be used across projects. They represent a technical solution such as the SQL Server environment, an App Service Environment, a messaging environment, or a data center comprising of virtual machines. The main template can then call **intermediate templates**, also known as **configuration templates**. The job of the intermediate templates is to compose leaf-level or single resource-level templates. These templates are called **known configuration templates** because they provide multiple options to the deployer. The deployer can choose from these options to create resources from these known configuration templates. For example, for creating a data center environment, the options provided could be small, medium, and large. Based on the value provided by the deployer, the template could provision a different number of virtual machines for small, medium, and large options. These options are also known as **SKUs** or **T-shirt sizes**.

These known configuration templates are created to provide flexibility to the deployer to create a different environment based on these SKUs, using the same ARM templates. This is shown in the next screenshot:

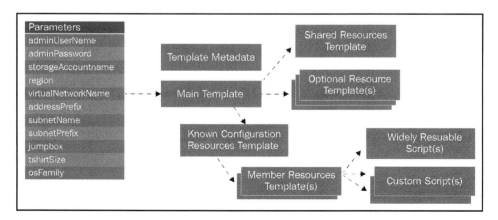

Design Patterns

Scenario

In this section, we will use a scenario to show the process of creating reusable and modular ARM templates. The scenario is actually quite simple. In this scenario, we would need an Azure SQL Server and a database that will be shared among multiple App Services Web Apps that are deployed across multiple regions and resource groups.

Some of the patterns demonstrated by means of this scenario are as follows:

- The templates are stored in an Azure storage account protected by SAS tokens
- Generating the subtemplate location URIs at runtime, for easy changes and maintenance
- Tagging each resource, including the resource groups
- Using the `copy` element to dynamically loop and create resources into multiple locations
- Resource group names, location, resource names, and their location determined dynamically, using parameters
- Usage of the `copy` element within the variables section, to generate variables dynamically
- Grouping of multiple parameters into a single parameter
- An existing Azure Key Vault contains the SAS token for accessing the storage container consisting of ARM templates
- Creating resource groups from a master template
- Usage of multiple nested ARM templates
- Creating an App Services plan and web apps in Western Europe and eastern US regions in separate resource groups, simultaneously
- Deploying SQL Server resources—SQL Server, SQL Database, and firewall rules, using a single template acting as a shared template
- The same Key Vault containing the storage SAS token also contains the password for Azure SQL Server
- Using the Key Vault resource statically for the storage account's SAS token
- Using the Key Vault resource dynamically for the Azure SQL password
- Passing the runtime information about Azure SQL to Azure App Services to generate the connection string at runtime

- Interdependencies among the resources in the ARM template
- Subtemplates implementing single resources such as the App Services plan and the web app
- Outputs from one template used in another template

Technical prerequisites

For implementing the scenario, there are a few technical requirements. We should have a resource group containing a storage account to store our ARM templates and an Azure Key Vault to store secrets related to the Azure SQL Server password and a storage account SAS token.

For information about creating Key Vaults and storage accounts using ARM templates, previous chapters should be referred to. In this section, we will create both these resources in a resource group, using Azure PowerShell.

Setting up Azure login and subscription

Before you can start creating resources in Azure, log into Azure. Open a new PowerShell console and type the next command shown:

```
Login-AzureRmAccount
```

It will pop open a new browser window and provide credentials to log into Azure. If everything goes well, you will log into the default subscription. Switch over to the preferred subscription in the case of the availability of multiple subscriptions, using this command:

```
Set-AzureRmContext -subscription <<Your subscription id or name>>
```

New resource group

So, now it's time to create a new resource group. The next shown command should be executed from the same console to create a new resource group named `ARMPatterns` in the Western European region:

```
New-AzureRmResourceGroup -Name "ARMPatterns" -Location "West Europe" -Verbose
```

[163]

Design Patterns

The output from this command should be the equivalent of what you see here:

```
PS C:\Users\rites> New-AzureRmResourceGroup -Name "ARMPatterns" -Location "West Europe" -Verbose
VERBOSE: Performing the operation "Replacing resource group ..." on target "ARMPatterns".
VERBOSE: 5:48:22 AM - Created resource group 'ARMPatterns' in location 'westeurope'


ResourceGroupName : ARMPatterns
Location          : westeurope
ProvisioningState : Succeeded
Tags              :
ResourceId        : /subscriptions/                              /resourceGroups/ARMPatterns
```

Creating an Azure Storage Account

After creating a resource group, we can now create a storage account within it. The storage account is needed for storing the ARM templates. These ARM templates will be reused and linked from another template. The command for creating the storage account is shown next, and the name should obviously be changed, because all the storage accounts should be uniquely named globally:

```
New-AzureRmStorageAccount -ResourceGroupName ARMPatterns -Name
"hostforarmtemplates" -SkuName Standard_LRS -Location "West Europe" -Kind
StorageV2 -AccessTier Hot -Verbose
```

If the command runs successfully, the output generated is shown next. If there are errors while creating the storage account, ensure that the name is unique:

```
StorageAccountName   ResourceGroupName   Location    SkuName       Kind       AccessTier   CreationTime              ProvisioningState   EnableHttpsTrafficOnly
------------------   -----------------   --------    -------       ----       ----------   ------------              -----------------   ----------------------
hostforarmtemplates  ARMPatterns         westeurope  StandardLRS   StorageV2  Hot          2019-02-08 10:48:46 AM    Succeeded           False
```

Creating an Azure Storage blob container

We also need to create a new blob container within the newly created storage account. The access to this container should be allowed only to authorized users. You should execute the next shown set of commands to create a new secure blob container. The first command declares a variable with the name of the container, and the next command creates a new container within the newly created storage account:

```
$containerName = "armtemplates"

New-AzureRmStorageContainer -ResourceGroupName ARMPatterns -
StorageAccountName "hostforarmtemplates"  -Name $containerName -
PublicAccess None -Verbose
```

[164]

Generating an Azure Storage SAS token

Next, we need to generate a new SAS token for the blob container, within the newly created storage account. The access to this container should be allowed only to authorized users supplying this SAS token along with their request. You should execute the next shown set of commands to create a new SAS token. The first command gets a reference to the newly created storage account. This is needed to obtain the security context used by the next command. The next command after it creates a new SAS token that expires within 100 days and only has read permission on the container and its constituent blob files:

```
$storage=Get-AzureRmStorageAccount -ResourceGroupNameARMPatterns-
Name"hostforarmtemplates"

New-AzureStorageContainerSASToken -Container $containerName -Context
$storage.Context -StartTime ([datetime]::Now) -ExpiryTime
([datetime]::Now.AddDays(100)) -Protocol HttpsOnly -Permission r -Verbose
```

The output from this command is the SAS token, which is displayed once and is not stored anywhere. You should make a note of the generated token and store it in a secure location. This SAS token will eventually be stored in an Azure Key Vault and used in ARM templates to access the subtemplates stored in this container. The generated SAS token is shown next:

```
?sv=2018-03-28&sr=c&sig=q47%2BlaoU8ZvrRmhrCR7iles3qoLhGMeu%2F4JXb8lwDdI%3D&
spr=https&st=2019-02-08T10%3A50%3A03Z&se=2019-05-19T09%3A50%3A03Z&sp=r
```

Uploading ARM templates to storage

Navigate to the Azure portal and to the blob storage and check whether the container is visible. Upload the following ARM templates files from the attached chapter code. These ARM templates are only accessible to the request that appends the generated SAS token to the URL request:

- appserviceplan-1.0.0.0.json
- webappsimple-1.0.0.0.json
- SharedServicesSQL-1.0.0.0.json

Design Patterns

As you can see in the following screenshot:

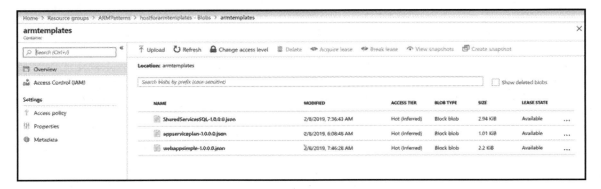

The URL for these ARM templates uses the pattern consisting of the account name, container name, and blob file name, and an example is shown here: `https://hostforarmtemplates.blob.core.windows.net/armtemplates/SharedServicesSQL-1.0.0.0.json`. However, just providing this URL will not enable access to the file and its content. To access these files, the URL should be appended to the SAS token, as shown next:

```
https://hostforarmtemplates.blob.core.windows.net/armtemplates/SharedServic
esSQL-1.0.0.0.json?sv=2018-03-28&sr=c&sig=q47%2BlaoU8ZvrRmhrCR7iles3qoLhGMe
u%2F4JXb8lwDdI%3D&spr=https&st=2019-02-08T10%3A50%3A03Z&se=2019-05-19T09%3A
50%3A03Z&sp=r
```

Creating an Azure Key Vault

The Azure Key Vault is created next, within the same resource group created earlier in this chapter. Please ensure that the Key Vault is enabled for deployment and template deployment. Enabling it for disk encryption, soft delete, and purge protection is optional in the current scenario.

The command for creating a new Key Vault using PowerShell is shown next:

```
New-AzureRmKeyVault -Name keyvaultarmtemplatebook -ResourceGroupName
ARMPatterns -Location "West Europe" -EnabledForDeployment -
EnabledForTemplateDeployment -EnabledForDiskEncryption -EnableSoftDelete -
EnablePurgeProtection -Sku Standard -Verbose
```

The result of the execution of the previous command is shown in the next screenshot:

You are advised to take note of the `Resource ID` generated as an output of the previous command. It would be used in other ARM templates to refer to this Key Vault.

Now that the Key Vault is created, we can create a couple of secrets and store them in this vault. These secrets are related to the SQL Server password and the Blob Storage SAS token.

Creating secrets in Key Vault

To create secrets in Azure Key Vault, execute the next set of commands for both the SQL Server password and the Storage SAS token. The first command stores the Storage SAS token, and it is valid for a year, from the time of creation. The secret should be converted into a secure string before storing it in Key Vault. The next command stores the SQL Server login password, and it is also valid for a year, from the time of creation. The secret should also be converted into a secure string before storing it in a Key Vault:

```
Set-AzureKeyVaultSecret -VaultName keyvaultarmtemplatebook -Name
"storageAccountkey" -SecretValue (ConvertTo-SecureString -String
"?sv=2018-03-28&sr=c&sig=q47%2BlaoU8ZvrRmhrCR7iles3qoLhGMeu%2F4JXb8lwDdI%3D
&spr=https&st=2019-02-08T10%3A50%3A03Z&se=2019-05-19T09%3A50%3A03Z&sp=r" -
AsPlainText -Force) -Expires ([datetime]::Now).AddYears(1) -Verbose
```

After storing the storage key in Azure Key Vault, we can now store the SQL Server password as well, within Azure Key Vault:

```
Set-AzureKeyVaultSecret -VaultName keyvaultarmtemplatebook -Name
"adminstratorPasswordSQL" -SecretValue (ConvertTo-SecureString -String
"citynext!1234" -AsPlainText  -Force) -Expires
([datetime]::Now).AddYears(1) -Verbose
```

Creating the Azure AD Service Principal

The newly created Key Vault can be accessed by the currently logged-in user; however, a better practice is to use Azure Service Principal to access the Key Vaults. Service Principal are very similar to service accounts that can be authenticated either using a password or a certificate. We also want our Key Vault to be accessed using a Service Principal rather than an individual account. Creating a new Azure Service Principal using PowerShell comprises multiple steps.

The first step is to create a new Service Application in Azure AD. A service application acts like a blueprint, based on which multiple Service Principal can be created.

To create a new Service Principal, the next command shown should be executed. It is to be noted that all the names mentioned in the next command should be replaced with your own names, as they should be unique. This command internally has a subcommand `ConvertTo-SecureString` to convert the plaintext password into a secure string. Secure strings are represented in base64 encoding:

```
$app = New-AzureRmADApplication -DisplayName
"https://keyvault.armtemplate.com" -IdentifierUris
"https://keyvault.armtemplate.com" -HomePage
"https://keyvault.armtemplate.com" -Password (ConvertTo-SecureString -
String sysadminpassword -AsPlainText  -Force) -Verbose
```

After creating the service application, a Service Principal can be created using the command as shown next. This command accepts a scope parameter to which the newly created Service Principal is applied, and a contributor role is assigned to it. `Contributor` role has read and write permissions. It is also possible to assign owner rights to the Service Principal. The Service Principal will expire after 1 year from its creation in this example:

```
New-AzureRmADServicePrincipal -ApplicationId $app.ApplicationId -
DisplayName "https://keyvault.armtemplate.com" -Password (ConvertTo-
SecureString -String sysadminpassword -AsPlainText  -Force) -Scope
"/subscriptions/b78602d4-6bd9-4fab-96ae-ed174be388dc" -Role Contributor -
StartDate ([datetime]::Now) -EndDate $([datetime]::now.AddYears(1)) -
Verbose
```

The output of the previous command is shown next:

```
ServicePrincipalNames : {..., https://keyvault.armtemplate.com}
ApplicationId         : 
DisplayName           : https://keyvault.armtemplate.com
Id                    : 
AdfsId                : 
Type                  : ServicePrincipal
```

Assigning permissions to a Service Principal on Key Vault

Now that the Service Principal has been created, we can assign permissions to it for enabling access to the Key Vault. This can be done by executing a command, as shown next. In this command, the object ID refers to the ID property generated as part of the creation of the Service Principal. The previous image consists of `Id` property that can be used as object ID in the next shown command. The next command assigns `get` and `list` permissions to the service principal on the Key Vault:

```
Set-AzureRmKeyVaultAccessPolicy -VaultName keyvaultarmtemplatebook -ResourceGroupName ARMPatterns -ObjectId "xxxxxxxx-xxxx-xxxx-xxxx-xxxxxxxxxxxx" -PermissionsToKeys get,list -PermissionsToCertificates get,list  -PermissionsToSecrets get,list -Verbose
```

The application ID generated in the last screenshot will be the user ID for login to Azure using the Service Principal approach, and the password is the same password that was used to create the Service Principal. We will use both the application ID and the password to log in to Azure later in this chapter for initiating deployment of ARM templates.

Deploying the solution

After enabling the technical prerequisites, we can deploy the master ARM template. This master template will use the subtemplates stored, on the Azure storage blob containers, to deploy the resources. The master template file and its parameters file are available with the chapter-accompanied code. The files that should be used for deploying the entire solution are as follows:

- `azuredeploy.json`
- `azuredeploy.parameters.json`

Both of these files can be stored on the location computer disk for execution. The `azuredeploy.json` file is the master template that linked all the other templates, and the `azuredeploy.parameters` file provides configuration information to the `azuredeploy.json` template. This configuration information is passed as parameters to the original template. The templates then use these values to create their own resources and also to supply them to the subtemplates, using the concept of linked templates. We have previously learned how to use linked templates in this book.

Log to Azure using Service Principal

Before you can start deploying resources on Azure using ARM template, we should log in to Azure using the newly created Service Principal. Open a new PowerShell console and type in the next set of shown commands. You should be replacing the value for username variable with the application ID of your Service Principal and the tenant ID with your Azure tenant ID. The password should be the same password used while creating the Service Principal.

```
$username = "xxxxxxxx-xxxx-xxxx-xxxx-xxxxxxxxxxxx"
$pass = "sysadminpassword"
$password = ConvertTo-SecureString -String $pass -AsPlainText -Force
$cred = New-Object System.Management.Automation.PSCredential -ArgumentList $username, $password
Login-AzureRmAccount -ServicePrincipal -Credential $cred -TenantId xxxxxxxx-xxxx-xxxx-xxxx-xxxxxxxxxxxx  -Verbose
```

If everything goes right, this time, there will be no pop-up Window, and loging in will happen silently. After this, we can deploy our ARM templates on to the Azure subscription.

Deploying the ARM template

To deploy the template, the `New-AzureRmDeployment` cmdlet is used. It is available from within the latest version. I am using version 6.6.0 of Azure PowerShell.

The `New-AzureRMDeployment` cmdlet is used when the template has also created resource groups. You should notice that no resource group information is provided in the next command. This is because the resource groups are created while deploying the ARM template, and all resources are deployed within those resource groups. A base location is provided for deploying the ARM template. This cmdlet also takes the name and path to the ARM template and its parameters file:

```
New-AzureRmDeployment -Name "test1" -TemplateFile
"C:\Users\rites\source\repos\AzureResourceGroup18\AzureResourceGroup18\azuredeploy.json" -TemplateParameterFile
"C:\Users\rites\source\repos\AzureResourceGroup18\AzureResourceGroup18\azuredeploy.parameters.json" -Location "West Europe" -Verbose
```

The template deployment a takes few minutes to finish, and the final outputs are shown next. The template creates two resource groups at deployment time:

The shared SQL Server and database is created in the `RGP-DEV-eCommerceUS` resource group. The region of this resource group is **East US 2**. This resource group also contains other resources related to the App Services plan and the web app:

One more resource group, `RGP-DEV-eCommerceEurope`, is created during template deployment in the **West Europe** region, and it just contains the App Service plan and the App Service web app:

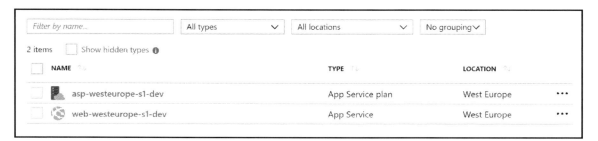

Template patterns

Templates should follow a few established patterns to make them more reusable, maintainable, and extensible. In this section, we will look into patterns that should be used for creating enterprise-grade templates. We will also look into some examples that use specific patterns to solve specific problems.

Modular ARM templates

Instead of declaring all resources within a single ARM template, the entire solution has been decomposed into multiple smaller ARM templates, each responsible for a single resource, or a group of related resources.

The single resource templates created after decomposition are these:

- `appserviceplan-1.0.0.0`
- `webappsimple-1.0.0.0`

The `appserviceplan-1.0.0.0` ARM template is responsible for creating an App Services plan. This plan is needed for creating a web app.

The `webappsimple-1.0.0.0` ARM template is responsible for creating an App Service web app. It uses the already created App Service plan.

Related resources can be grouped together that share the same life cycle in terms of provisioning and deprovisioning. The `SharedServicesSQL-1.0.0.0` ARM template consists of multiple resources all related to Azure SQL. These resources include SQL Server, SQL Database, and SQL firewalls.

The `SharedServicesSQL-1.0.0.0` is also a shared template that can be used not only within the current scenario but also by other projects. Any project that needs to provision Azure SQL can use this template as is, by providing configuration information.
The `SharedServicesSQL-1.0.0.0` ARM template can also be thought of as a technical capability template that provisions a capability completely. An example of such a capability would be a virtual machine template comprising of multiple related resources such as a public IP address, a network interface card, storage accounts, and so on.

Let's go through these subtemplates and understand their code.

Generalized templates

Parameters and variables help with creating generalized templates. These are templates that can be used on multiple occasions in different projects. All the three subtemplates are generalized templates that accept important parameters for configuration.

Azure SQL template

The Parameters `SharedServicesSQL-1.0.0.0` ARM template is as follows:

```
"parameters": {
    "administratorLogin": { "type": "string" },
    "administratorLoginPassword": { "type": "securestring" },
    "databaseName": { "type": "string" },
    "sqlserverName": {  "type": "string" },
    "customTags": { "type": "object" },
    "collation": {
      "type": "string",
      "defaultValue": "SQL_Latin1_General_CP1_CI_AS"
    },
    "edition": {
      "type": "string",
      "defaultValue": "Basic",
      "allowedValues": [
        "Basic",
        "Standard",
        "Premium"
      ]
    },
    "maxSizeBytes": {
      "type": "string",
      "defaultValue": "1073741824"
    },
    "requestedServiceObjectiveName": {
      "type": "string",
      "defaultValue": "Basic",
      "allowedValues": [
        "Basic",
        "S0",
        "S1",
        "S2",
        "P1",
        "P2",
        "P3"
      ],
      "metadata": {
        "description": "Describes the performance level for Edition"
      }
    }
  },
```

Design Patterns

The resources in this template include three related resources. The resource is responsible for creating an SQL Server. The code for this resource is listed next:

```
"name": "[parameters('sqlserverName')]",
      "type": "Microsoft.Sql/servers",
      "location": "[resourceGroup().location]",
      "tags": {
        "displayName": "SqlServer"
      },
      "apiVersion": "2014-04-01-preview",
      "properties": {
        "administratorLogin": "[parameters('administratorLogin')]",
        "administratorLoginPassword":
"[parameters('administratorLoginPassword')]"
      },
```

Notice how the password that is retrieved from the Key Vault is sent as a parameter to this template and assigned to the `administratorLoginPassword` property. The `Microsoft.Sql/servers` resource has two child resources. The first one is the database resource:

```
{
            "name": "[parameters('databaseName')]",
            "type": "databases",
            "location": "[resourceGroup().location]",
            "tags": {
              "displayName": "Database"
            },
            "apiVersion": "2014-04-01-preview",
            "dependsOn": [
              "[resourceId('Microsoft.Sql/servers/',
parameters('sqlserverName'))]"
            ],
            "properties": {
              "edition": "[parameters('edition')]",
              "collation": "[parameters('collation')]",
              "maxSizeBytes": "[parameters('maxSizeBytes')]",
              "requestedServiceObjectiveName":
"[parameters('requestedServiceObjectiveName')]"
            }
          },
```

The other one is the `firewallrules` resource:

```
{
        "type": "firewallrules",
        "apiVersion": "2014-04-01-preview",
        "dependsOn": [
          "[resourceId('Microsoft.Sql/servers/',
parameters('sqlserverName'))]"
        ],
        "location": "[resourceGroup().location]",
        "name": "AllowAllWindowsAzureIps",
        "properties": {
          "endIpAddress": "0.0.0.0",
          "startIpAddress": "0.0.0.0"
        }
      }
```

App service plan template

The `parameters` for the `appserviceplan-1.0.0.0` ARM template are as follows:

```
"parameters": {
  "customTags": { "type": "object" },
  "appServicePlanName": { "type": "string" },
  "appServicePlanSkuTier": { "type": "string" },
  "appServicePlanSkuName": { "type": "string" }
},
```

And the resources for this template include a single resource of type `Microsoft.Web/serverfarms`. This resource is responsible for creating an App Service plan. The code for this resource is listed next:

```
{
   "type": "Microsoft.Web/serverfarms",
   "kind": "app",
   "name": "[parameters('appServicePlanName')]",
   "location": "[resourceGroup().location]",
   "apiVersion": "2016-09-01",
   "tags": "[parameters('customTags')]",
   "properties": {
     "name": "[parameters('appServicePlanName')]"
   },
   "sku": {
     "Tier": "[parameters('appServicePlanSkuTier')]",
     "Name": "[parameters('appServicePlanSkuName')]"
   }
}
```

Design Patterns

Notice how all the important properties are provided values from parameters. This makes this template generic and reusable.

Azure App Services template

The parameters for the `webappsimple-1.0.0.0` ARM template are as follows:

```
"parameters": {
    "appServicePlanName": { "type": "string" },
    "diagnosticlevel": {
      "type": "string",
      "allowedValues": [ "error", "warning", "information", "verbose" ],
      "defaultValue": "warning"
    },
    "customTags": { "type": "object" },
    "webAppName": { "type": "string" },
    "serverName": { "type": "string" },
    "databaseName": { "type": "string" },
    "userID": { "type": "string" },
    "administratorLoginPassword": { "type": "securestring" }
},
```

And the resources for this template include a single resource of type `Microsoft.Web/sites`.

This resource is responsible for creating an App Service web app. The code for this resource is listed next:

```
{
"type": "Microsoft.Web/sites",
"kind": "app",
"name": "[parameters('webAppName')]",
"location": "[resourceGroup().location]",
"apiVersion": "2016-08-01",
"tags": "[parameters('customTags')]",
"properties": {
  "name": "[parameters('webAppName')]",
  "enabled": true,
  "reserved": true,
  "serverFarmId": "[resourceId('Microsoft.Web/serverFarms', parameters('appServicePlanName'))]",
      "siteConfig": {
        "AlwaysOn": true,
        "connectionStrings": [
          {
            "name": "ConnString1",
```

```
                "connectionString": "[concat('Data Source=tcp:',
parameters('serverName'), 'Initial Catalog=', parameters('databaseName'),
'User Id=', parameters('userID') , 'Password=',
parameters('administratorLoginPassword') , ';')]"
              }
            ]
          },
          "applicationLogs": {
            "fileSystem": {
              "level": "On"
            },
            "azureTableStorage": {
              "level": "Off",
              "sasUrl": null
            }
          },
          "httpLogs": {
            "fileSystem": {
              "retentionInMb": 35,
              "retentionInDays": 365,
              "enabled": false
            }
          },
          "failedRequestsTracing": {
            "enabled": true
          },
          "detailedErrorMessages": {
            "enabled": true
          }
        }
      }
```

Again, notice how all the important properties are provided values from parameters. Also, it is important to note that this resource should be related to an App Service plan. The code listed shown in bold uses the parameter `appServicePlanName` to generate the resource ID using the `resourceId` function.

Another important aspect to notice in the previous code listing is the generation of `connectionstring`. We have created an SQL Server environment, and the web app should be able to connect to it using `connectionstring`. The values are concatenated together to generate the connection string. All values are used from parameters for this purpose.

Design Patterns

All these three templates are subtemplates that are used by a master template, by linking them.

The master template uses a specialized resource called `Microsoft.Resources/deployments` that can invoke linked templates that are stored elsewhere—generally, on Azure storage accounts.

The master template consists of three such deployment resources, one for invoking each `appserviceplan-1.0.0.0`, `webappsimple-1.0.0.0`, and `SharedServicesSQL-1.0.0.0` ARM templates.

Apart from invoking these subtemplates, it also declared a resource for creating resource groups. Let's dive into the code of the `azuredeploy.json` master template.

The parameters for the `azuredeploy.json` master arm template are as follows:

```
"parameters": {
    "resourceGroupInfo": { "type": "array" },
    "sqlServerProperties": { "type": "object" },
    "environmentName": {
      "type": "string",
      "allowedValues": [ "DEV", "TST", "PRD", "SIT", "PAT", "STG", "UAT" ]
    },
    "department": { "type": "string" },
    "templateRepository": { "type": "object" },
    "storagekey": { "type": "securestring"  },
    "appServicePlanSkuTier": { "type": "string"  },
    "appServicePlanSkuName": { "type": "string" },
    "diagnosticlevel": { "type": "string" }
},
```

The parameters are self-explanatory; however, the variables section needs elaborating. Some of the variables in this template are shown next. The variables are used to generate the file location, including the storage key from the Key Vault. The resources in this ARM template use these file locations as linked templates. Key Vaults are discussed in the next section of this chapter:

```
"templateRefBaseUri": "[concat('https://',
parameters('templateRepository').libraryTemplateStorageAccountName,'.blob.c
ore.windows.net/',
parameters('templateRepository').libraryTemplateStorageContainerName,
'/')]",

"templateRefAppPlanTemplateUri": "[concat(variables('templateRefBaseUri'),
'appserviceplan-1.0.0.0.json',parameters('storagekey'))]",
```

```
"templateRefWebAppTemplateUri": "[concat(variables('templateRefBaseUri'),
'webappsimple-1.0.0.0.json',parameters('storagekey'))]",

"templateRefSharedServicesTemplateUri":
"[concat(variables('templateRefBaseUri'),
'SharedServicesSQL-1.0.0.0.json',parameters('storagekey'))]",
```

The template first creates multiple resource groups based on the `resourceGroupInfo` parameter:

```
{
   "type": "Microsoft.Resources/resourceGroups",
   "location":
"[parameters('resourceGroupInfo')[copyIndex()].resourceGroupLocation]",
   "name":
"[variables('multiLocation').location[copyIndex()].resourceGroupName]",
   "apiVersion": "2018-05-01",
   "tags": "[variables('variableTags')]",
   "copy": {
     "name": "allResourceGroups",
     "count": "[length(parameters('resourceGroupInfo'))]"
   },
   "properties": {}
},
```

The parameters file contains values for this `resourceGroupInfo` parameter object:

```
"resourceGroupInfo": {
    "value": [
       {
         "resourceGroupName": "eCommerceUS",
         "resourceGroupLocation": "East US 2",
         "resourceGroupSuffix": "eastus"
       },
       {
         "resourceGroupName": "eCommerceEurope",
         "resourceGroupLocation": "West Europe",
         "resourceGroupSuffix": "westEurope"
       }
    ]
},
```

Design Patterns

This parameter contains two objects: one for the resource group in the eastern US and the other in Western Europe. Using this information, the template loops through these objects and creates a resource group for each object. Since there are two objects, two resource groups are created. If we add another object, an additional resource group will be created.

The next resource is to deploy the `SharedServicesSQL-1.0.0.0` template using the linked template feature. It uses the `Microsoft.Resources/deployments` resource type and deploys in the first resource group:

```
        {
          "type": "Microsoft.Resources/deployments",
          "apiVersion": "2017-05-10",
          "name": "sharedServices-sqlServices",
          "resourceGroup":
"[variables('multiLocation').location[0].resourceGroupName]",
          "dependsOn": [ "allResourceGroups" ],
          "properties": {
            "mode": "Incremental",
            "templateLink": {
              "uri": "[variables('templateRefSharedServicesTemplateUri')]",
              "contentVersion": "1.0.0.0"
            },
            "parameters": {
              "administratorLogin":{ "value":
"[parameters('sqlServerProperties').administratorLogin]"},
              "administratorLoginPassword": {
                "reference": {
                  "keyVault": {
                    "id": "[concat(subscription().id,'/resourcegroups/',
parameters('sqlServerProperties').keyVaultResourceGroupName,
'/providers/Microsoft.KeyVault/vaults/',
parameters('sqlServerProperties').keyVaultName)]"
                  },
                  "secretName":
"[parameters('sqlServerProperties').adminstratorPasswordSecretName]"
                }
              },
              "databaseName": { "value":
"[parameters('sqlServerProperties').databaseName]" },
              "customTags": { "value": "[variables('variableTags')]" },
              "collation": { "value":
"[parameters('sqlServerProperties').collation]" },
              "edition": {  "value":
"[parameters('sqlServerProperties').edition]" },
              "maxSizeBytes": {  "value":
"[parameters('sqlServerProperties').maxSizeBytes]" },
              "requestedServiceObjectiveName": {
```

```
            "value":
"[parameters('sqlServerProperties').requestedServiceObjectiveName]" },
        "sqlserverName": {   "value":
"[parameters('sqlServerProperties').sqlserverName]" }
        }
      }
    }
```

The code listing for deploying the `appserviceplan-1.0.0.0` template using the linked template is shown next:

```
    {
      "type": "Microsoft.Resources/deployments",
      "apiVersion": "2017-05-10",
      "name": "[concat('crossAppServePlan', copyIndex())]",
      "dependsOn": [
        "sharedServices-sqlServices"
      ],
      "copy": {
        "name": "allAppServicePlans",
        "count": "[length(parameters('resourceGroupInfo'))]"
      },
      "resourceGroup":
"[variables('multiLocation').location[copyIndex()].resourceGroupName]",
      "properties": {
        "mode": "Incremental",
        "templateLink": {
          "uri": "[variables('templateRefAppPlanTemplateUri')]",
          "contentVersion": "1.0.0.0"
        },
        "parameters": {
          "appServicePlanName": {
            "value":
"[variables('multiLocation').location[copyIndex()].appServicePlanName]"
          },
          "appServicePlanSkuTier": {
            "value": "[parameters('appServicePlanSkuTier')]"
          },
          "appServicePlanSkuName": {
            "value": "[parameters('appServicePlanSkuName')]"
          },
          "customTags": {
            "value": "[variables('variableTags')]"
          }
        }
      }
    },
```

Design Patterns

The listing for deploying the `webappsimple-1.0.0.0` template the linked template is shown next:

```
    {
      "type": "Microsoft.Resources/deployments",
      "apiVersion": "2017-05-10",
      "name": "[concat('crossWebApp', copyIndex())]",
      "dependsOn": [ "allAppServicePlans" ],
      "copy": {
        "name": "allWebApps",
        "count": "[length(parameters('resourceGroupInfo'))]"
      },
      "resourceGroup": "[variables('multiLocation').location[copyIndex()].resourceGroupName]",
      "properties": {
        "mode": "Incremental",
        "templateLink": {
          "uri": "[variables('templateRefWebAppTemplateUri')]",
          "contentVersion": "1.0.0.0"
        },
        "parameters": {
          "appServicePlanName": {
            "value": "[variables('multiLocation').location[copyIndex()].appServicePlanName]"
          },
          "diagnosticlevel": { "value": "[parameters('diagnosticlevel')]"
},
          "webAppName":{"value": "[variables('multiLocation').location[copyIndex()].webAppName]" },
          "serverName"{
    "value": "[concat(reference('sharedServices-sqlServices').outputs.SQLServerFQDN.value,', 1433;')]"
          },
          "databaseName":{"value":"[concat(parameters('sqlServerProperties').databaseName,'; ')]" },
          "userID": {
"value":"[concat(parameters('sqlServerProperties').administratorLogin,'; ')]" },
          "customTags": { "value": "[variables('variableTags')]" },
          "administratorLoginPassword": {
            "reference": {
              "keyVault": {
                "id": "[concat('/subscriptions/9755ffce-e94b-4332-9be8-1ade15e78909','/resourcegroups/',parameters('sqlServerProperties').keyVaultResourceGroupName,'/providers/Microsoft.KeyVault/vaults/',parameters('sqlServerProperties').keyVaultName)]"
              },
```

```
                "secretName":
"[parameters('sqlServerProperties').adminstratorPasswordSecretName]"
            }
          }
        }
      }
    }
```

Using Key Vault for passwords and secrets

The Key Vault is used for the storage of the SAS token and the SQL login password. There should not be any secrets, keys, and passwords available, either within the ARM templates or their associated parameters file. These passwords and secrets should be pulled from Key Vault at runtime and used for configuring the resource. In this case, our subtemplates are protected using the SAS token that is stored in the Key Vault. We will not be able to run the master template unless we retrieve the SAS token from the Key Vault and supply it to the master template.

Static usage of Key Vault information

The storage SAS token used the static reference to the Key Vault. *Static* here means that the Key Vault identifier is fixed in the parameters file and the ARM template does not have any control to use any other Key Vault. The master template has a parameter defined as follows:

```
"storagekey": {
   "type": "securestring"
},
```

The parameter is of type `securestring`. Secure strings are not written to log entries generated during the deployment of templates. Anybody reading the log files will not be able to ascertain the storage SAS token.

It means the template is expecting the storage key to be supplied from the parameter file. Within the parameters file, the parameter is supplied after retrieving the secret from the Key Vault. The code in the parameters file is responsible for fetching the storage SAS token. The `storageAccountKey` is shown next. Notice that instead of providing a hardcoded value, a reference is used.

Design Patterns

The reference is pointing to the Azure Key Vault using the same resource ID that we generated while creating the Key Vault. Along with the identifier for the Key Vault, we also supply the identifier to retrieve the value from the `storageAccountKey` secret:

```
"storagekey": {
  "reference": {
    "keyVault": { "id": "/subscriptions/9755ffce-e94b-4332-9be8-1ade15e78909/resourceGroups/ARMPatterns/providers/Microsoft.KeyVault/vaults/keyvaultarmtemplatebook" },
    "secretName": "storageAccountkey"
  }
},
```

This storage key is then used within the variable section to generate the complete sub-template URLs by appending to the original blob files, as shown here. Notice the first variable creates the base subtemplate location URI using the storage account and the container name. Both values are also supplied as `templateRepository` parameters. This parameter is of an object type, and it can accept arbitrary JSON objects:

```
"templateRepository": {
    "type": "object"
},

"templateRefBaseUri": "[concat('https://',parameters('templateRepository').libraryTemplateStorageAccountName,'.blob.core.windows.net/',parameters('templateRepository').libraryTemplateStorageContainerName,'/')]",

"templateRefAppPlanTemplateUri": "[concat(variables('templateRefBaseUri'),'appserviceplan-1.0.0.0.json',parameters('storagekey'))]",
```

Also notice how the storage key is appended to the template file URI using the `concat` function provided by ARM templates.

The `parameters` file supplies the values for the `templateRepository` parameter, and it is shown here:

```
    "templateRepository": {
  "value": {
    "libraryTemplateStorageAccountName": "hostforarmtemplates",
    "libraryTemplateStorageContainerName": "armtemplates"
  }
},
```

[184]

Chapter 7

 The values for `libraryTemplateStorageAccountName` and `libraryTemplateStorageContainerName` JSON element matches the storage account and the container we created as part of the technical prerequisites.

The resources use linked templates and refer to subtemplates stored in the storage account. The resource that creates the App Service plan is configured to use the variable `templateRefAppPlanTemplateUri` to refer to the linked template:

```
      {
        "type": "Microsoft.Resources/deployments",
        "apiVersion": "2017-05-10",
        "name": "[concat('crossAppServePlan', copyIndex())]",
        "dependsOn": [ "sharedServices-sqlServices" ],
        "copy": {
          "name": "allAppServicePlans",
          "count": "[length(parameters('resourceGroupInfo'))]"
        },
        "resourceGroup":
"[variables('multiLocation').location[copyIndex()].resourceGroupName]",
        "properties": {
          "mode": "Incremental",
          "templateLink": {
            "uri": "[variables('templateRefAppPlanTemplateUri')]",
            "contentVersion": "1.0.0.0"
          },
          "parameters": {
            "appServicePlanName": {
              "value":
"[variables('multiLocation').location[copyIndex()].appServicePlanName]"
            },
            "appServicePlanSkuTier": { "value":
"[parameters('appServicePlanSkuTier')]" },
            "appServicePlanSkuName": { "value":
"[parameters('appServicePlanSkuName')]" },
            "customTags": { "value": "[variables('variableTags')]" }
          }
        }
      },
```

Design Patterns

Dynamic declaration of Key Vault information

Instead of using the information to retrieve the secret from the Key Vault from the `parameters` file, secrets from the Key Vault can be retrieved dynamically within a template. The template will need the name of the Key Vault, the resource group containing the Key Vault, and the secret name. We want to pull the SQL Server login password from the Key Vault while creating the SQL Server resource during the deployment of the ARM template. The SQL Server template needs this password for the creation of the SQL resource. So, instead of declaring the Key Vault reference in the `parameters` file, we will instead provide parameters in the `parameters` file that represent the name of the resource group containing the Key Vault, Key Vault name, and the secret name, as shown here. These parameters are part of SQL Server-related parameters:

```
"sqlServerProperties": {
    "value": {
      "administratorLogin": "eCommerceAdmin",
      "databaseName": "eCommerceDatabase",
      "collation": "SQL_Latin1_General_CP1_CI_AS",
      "edition": "Standard",
      "maxSizeBytes": "1073741824",
      "requestedServiceObjectiveName": "S0",
      "sqlserverName": "armtemplatebooksqlserver",
      "keyVaultName": "keyvaultarmtemplatebook",
      "keyVaultResourceGroupName": "ARMPatterns",
      "adminstratorPasswordSecretName": "adminstratorPasswordSQL"
   }
}
```

The resource group name is `ARMPatterns`, and the name of the Key Vault is `KeyVaultarmtemplatebook`, and the secret name ID is `administratorPasswordSQL`.

These values are supplied to the master template file `azuredeploy.json`, as shown here. The parameter is of the object datatype:

```
"sqlServerProperties": {
  "type": "object"
},
```

Now the values from this parameter object can be used by the linked template deployment responsible for creating the Azure SQL Server:

```
{
  "type": "Microsoft.Resources/deployments",
  "apiVersion": "2017-05-10",
  "name": "sharedServices-sqlServices",
  "resourceGroup":
"[variables('multiLocation').location[0].resourceGroupName]",
```

```
      "dependsOn": [ "allResourceGroups" ],
      "properties": {
        "mode": "Incremental",
        "templateLink": {
          "uri": "[variables('templateRefSharedServicesTemplateUri')]",
          "contentVersion": "1.0.0.0"
        },
        "parameters": {
          "administratorLogin": { "value":
"[parameters('sqlServerProperties').administratorLogin]" },
          "administratorLoginPassword": {
            "reference": {
              "keyVault": {
                "id": "[concat(subscription().id,'/resourcegroups/',
parameters('sqlServerProperties').keyVaultResourceGroupName,
'/providers/Microsoft.KeyVault/vaults/',
parameters('sqlServerProperties').keyVaultName)]"
              },
              "secretName":
"[parameters('sqlServerProperties').adminstratorPasswordSecretName]"
            }
          },
          "databaseName": { "value":
"[parameters('sqlServerProperties').databaseName]" },
          "customTags":    { "value": "[variables('variableTags')]" },
          "collation":     { "value":
"[parameters('sqlServerProperties').collation]" },
          "edition": {        "value":
"[parameters('sqlServerProperties').edition]    },
          "maxSizeBytes": {  "value":
"[parameters('sqlServerProperties').maxSizeBytes]"   },
"requestedServiceObjectiveName": {
            "value":
"[parameters('sqlServerProperties').requestedServiceObjectiveName]"
          },
          "sqlserverName": { "value":
"[parameters('sqlServerProperties').sqlserverName]" }
        }
      }
    },
```

Design Patterns

Notice the previously listed code in bold. The code is similar to the code in the previous example using the Key Vault reference in the `parameters` file. However, this time, we can generate the Key Vault identifier at runtime, using the `concat` function. Also, note that the `concat` function generates a resource identifier in this format:

```
/subscriptions/{subscriptionId}/resourcegroups/{resourceGroupName}/providers/{resourceProviderNamespace}/{resourceType}/{resourceName}
```

It is also possible to use the `resourceId` function provided by the ARM templates to generate this Key Vault identifier. Also, note the usage of the `secretName`. It is provided from the `sqlServerProperties` object.

The `sqlServerProperties` parameter will also be used for configuring the `connectionstring` in the Azure app services web app configuration that we will see later in this chapter.

Dependencies between resources

The ARM templates consist of multiple resources and, by default, all these resources are designed to be provisioned in parallel. If there is a need to sequence the creation of these resources, the author of these templates needs to define the **Dependencies** between these resources explicitly. With the help of the `dependsOn` element within a resource, a dependency can be defined. An example of the **Dependencies** among resources is shown in the next diagram for a **Virtual Machine** resource. From the screenshot, it is evident that the **Dependencies** features are being used in the wrong way. Here, the **Virtual Network** depends on the **Storage Account**, and the **Network Interface Card** (**NIC**) depends on both the **Storage Account** and the **Virtual Network**, while the **Virtual Machine** depends on all three resources—the **Storage Account**, the **Virtual Network**, and the **Network Interface Card**:

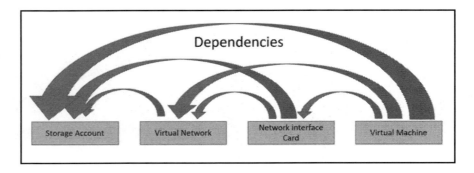

A better way to declare **Dependencies** among resources is shown in the next diagram. Here, there is no dependency between a **Virtual Network** and a **Storage Account**, and the NIC depends on the **Virtual Network** resource, and the **Virtual Machine** is dependent on the **Storage Account** and the NIC. Eventually, by the nature of the interdependency among the resources, the **Virtual Machine** will only be provisioned after all three resources are provisioned. Both the **Storage Account** and the **Virtual Network** are provisioned in parallel after the creation of the **Virtual Network** resource; the NIC is provisioned, and finally after the provision of both the **Storage Account** and the NIC, the **Virtual Machine** resource is provisioned. This is shown in the next diagram:

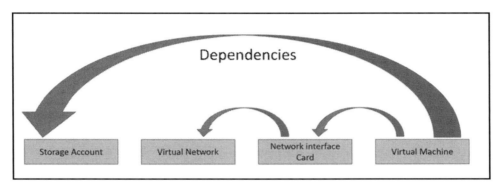

Declaring **Dependencies** in this way makes the process faster and smoother. Even changing and maintaining ARM templates is easier, since multiple changes among **Dependencies** is avoided. In the current scenario, the **Dependencies** among the four resources are depicted in the next diagram:

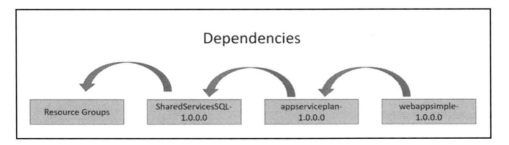

Creating multiple resources in loop

We already know how to use the `copy` feature of the ARM templates to loop and create resources. Azure provides the capability to use even the `copy` features in the variables as well.

The variables defined within the `variables` section of the ARM templates are static in their count. If you define five variables, you get just five variables. Earlier, there was no way to have a dynamic number of variables during deployment. Adding `copy` into the variables helps with achieving defined variables at runtime and using them in ARM templates.

There are two distinct ways to use the `copy` element within the variables section. The first one generates a JSON object containing an array, while the other generates an array. If the `copy` element appears at the top level as a variable, it generates an array and assigns it to a variable generated during deployment. The name of the variable is the value provided to the `name` property. When the `copy` keyword is used as within a variable name, it generates an object, and creates an inner variable, assigning an array to it.

If you look at the master template `azuredeploy.json`, you will notice the `copy` feature used in the `variables` section, as shown here:

```
"multiLocation": {
    "copy": [
        {
            "name": "location",
            "count": "[length(parameters('resourceGroupInfo'))]",
            "input": {
                "resourceGroupName": "[concat('RGP','-',parameters('environmentName'),'-',parameters('resourceGroupInfo')[copyIndex('location')].resourceGroupName)]",
                "appServicePlanName": "[toLower(concat('asp','-',parameters('resourceGroupInfo')[copyIndex('location')].resourceGroupSuffix,'-',parameters('appServicePlanSkuName'),'-',parameters('environmentName')))]",
                "webAppName": "[toLower(concat('web','-',parameters('resourceGroupInfo')[copyIndex('location')].resourceGroupSuffix,'-', parameters('appServicePlanSkuName'),'-',parameters('environmentName')))]"
            }
        }
    ]
}
```

The variable `multiLocation` does not have a static value; instead, it uses the `copy` feature. When the `copy` keyword is used, as within the `multiLocation` variable, it generates an object and creates an inner variable named `location`, assigning an array to it. The array comprises of the values generated from the `input` values.

In the current sample, the length of the `resourceGroupInfo` object supplied as the parameter is 2. It means the `copy` element loops twice and generates two objects within a new array. The objects would contain values as shown here:

```
"multiLocation": {
    "location": [
        {
            "resourceGroupName": "RGP-Dev-eCommerceUS",
            "appServicePlanName": "asp-eastus-S1-DEV",
            "webAppName": "web-eastus-S1-DEV"
        },
        {
            "resourceGroupName": "RGP-Dev-eCommerceEurope",
            "appServicePlanName": "asp-westEurope-S1-DEV",
            "webAppName": "web-westEurope-S1-DEV"
        }
    ]
}
```

The `length` function, when applied to an array, provides the `count` of the element. The `concat` function joins multiple string values together. The parameter value `DEV` was provided for the `environmentName` and `S1` for the `appServicePlanSkuName`.

Two objects were generated at runtime that can be referenced within the ARM template, using the syntax as shown here. The syntax accesses the `resourceGroupName`-generated property, using the `location` array:

```
"[variables('multiLocation').location[copyIndex()].resourceGroupName]"
```

This pattern should be used whenever there is a need to generate multiple variables at runtime, rather than defining them statically at design time.

Tagging of resources

Every resource including the resource groups are tagged in the ARM template. Tags help with the categorization of resources, and this helps with generating multiple types of reports, by slicing and dicing the logs generated by Azure, to gain insights into them. For example, `tags` can help in providing costs and usage information based on environments, departments, and other categories if the user provides this information as custom `tags` to the resources. It is a good design to tag resources and resource groups.

Tags are assigned to resources using the `tags` element. The `tags` can be assigned statically, as shown here:

```
"tags": {
  "department": "Finance",
  "environment": "Development",
  "resourceType" :  "resource group"
},
```

In the current scenario, however, `tags` are not assigned statically. The values for `tags` are provided as parameters, as shown in the listing here:

```
"environmentName": {
  "type": "string",
  "allowedValues": [ "DEV", "TST", "PRD", "SIT", "PAT", "STG", "UAT" ]
},
"department": {
  "type": "string"
},
```

These `parameters` are used in `variables` to generate the tag value:

```
"variableTags": "[json(concat('{\"application\": \"All\", \"environment\":
\"',parameters('environmentName'),'\", \"supportTeam\":
\"',parameters('department'),'\"}'))]",
```
And then the variable "variableTags" is assigned to tags element in in all the resources as shown here.
```
    "tags": "[variables('variableTags')]",
```

Runtime sharing of property values

While deploying templates, at times, it is not possible to provide all the information needed by the resources. For example, a template might contain resources related to the Azure SQL and the Azure App Services web app. The web app needs information about the SQL Server FQDN that is only generated by deploying the SQL resource. This information is not available at design time before deploying the template. Another example is a template containing resources related to the dynamic public IP address, the virtual machine, and the SQL Server. The virtual machine should be assigned the IP address generated dynamically, and the same IP address should be whitelisted in the Azure SQL firewall rules. However, the IP address is not known at deployment time. The IP address will only be generated during the deployment of an IP address resource.

ARM templates can be designed in which runtime values generated by a resource can be passed dynamically to other resources.

In the current scenario, Azure App Services need SQL Server FQDN information to generate the `connectionString` used for connecting app services to Azure SQL.

In this design, the sub-template related to Azure SQL should generate an output containing the FQDN of the newly created SQL Server:

```
"outputs": {
    "SQLServerFQDN": {
       "type": "string",
       "value":
"[reference(parameters('sqlserverName')).fullyQualifiedDomainName]"
    }
}
```

The output from one template can be used to configure another template. However, to use the output of a template or a resource, `reference` should be used. This function takes one parameter, and that is the name of a resource. The resource could be of the deployment type in the case of a subtemplate.

Design Patterns

Within the given scenario, in a master template (`azuredeploy.json`), the App Services web app (sites) resource and the `serverName` parameter are supplied with values obtained from the output of the subtemplate. The resources in the subtemplate are not available for access directly. To access the outputs of the subtemplate, a reference to the deployment resource type should be made to obtain the outputs and the values within. This is shown in the next listing:

```
"serverName": {
  "value": "[concat(reference('sharedServices-
sqlServices').outputs.SQLServerFQDN.value,', 1433;')]"
        },
```

Redefining resources in the same template

By now, you already know that it is not possible to define two resources in the same template having the same name. This means that if we define a resource in the template and later in the deployment execution we want to change any of its configurations, then it is not possible to do this.

The first question that might arise is why we cannot configure the resource with the end state, rather than reconfiguring. This is because there are situations, as we learned in the previous section, where it might not be possible to have all the values at the time of deployment; however, as template execution progresses and resources generate additional information, some of the resources might need reconfiguration.

Let's understand this concept with the help of an example. Imagine we are creating a virtual machine using templates on an existing virtual network. We want to assign a static private IP address to this virtual machine. Since it is an existing virtual network that may already consist of virtual machines, we cannot determine the private IP that should be statically assigned to this virtual machine unless we query the virtual network for the next available private IP address. ARM templates do not have a mechanism to only query a resource. So, what is the solution?

There are two designs that can be used for such problems. These relate to using linked templates and nested templates.

Using the same example as before, one of the solutions would be to declare an NIC resource in a template configured to have a dynamic private IP address. Using a dynamic private IP address will ensure that we do not have to provide a static IP address as a parameter to the template. After the private IP address is assigned to the NIC belonging to the virtual machine, it is possible to get the output of the NIC, including the newly assigned private IP address, using the references function and invoke another template that has the same definition as the previous NIC, with the only difference being that it uses a static private IP address instead of a dynamic private IP address and assigns the IP address that was obtained by the reference function. The IP address obtained from the reference function is sent as a parameter to the linked template.

Another solution would be to use a nested template instead of a linked template. Using the design of a nested template, it is possible to change a resource configuration within the same template using the same name. The solution for this design is available in the `redefiningproperties.json` ARM template accompanied with the chapter code. The `parameters` for this ARM template are shown next. This template accepts two mandatory `parameters` related to the virtual network address range and the subnet address range:

```
"parameters": {
   "vnetAddressPrefix": {
     "type": "string",
     "metadata": {
       "description": "Address Prefix of the virtual network"
     }
   },
   "subnetPrefix": {
     "type": "string",
     "metadata": {
       "description": "address prefix of the subnet"
     }
   }
},
```

The `variables` section declares `variables` related to the naming of resources within the template. The last parameter is the resource identifier of the subnet. It is needed while declaring and associating an NIC to a subnet:

```
"variables": {
   "virtualNetworkName": "sampleVirtualNetwork",
   "subnetName": "FirstSubnet",
   "nicName": "nic1",
   "subnetRef": "[resourceId('Microsoft.Network/virtualNetworks/subnets', variables('virtualNetworkName'), variables('subnetName'))]"
 },
```

Design Patterns

There are three top-level resources within the template. The first resource is the virtual network, and its configuration is shown next. The name of the virtual network is read from the `virtualNetworkName` variable, and it is deployed to the same region as that of the resource group, and both the address range for the network and the subnet is assigned from the supplied `parameters`:

```
{
    "apiVersion": "2018-08-01",
    "type": "Microsoft.Network/virtualNetworks",
    "name": "[variables('virtualNetworkName')]",
    "location": "[resourceGroup().location]",
    "properties": {
      "addressSpace": {
        "addressPrefixes": [
          "[parameters('vnetAddressPrefix')]"
        ]
      },
      "subnets": [
        {
          "name": "[variables('subnetName')]",
          "properties": {
            "addressPrefix": "[parameters('subnetPrefix')]"
          }
        }
      ]
    }
},
```

The next resource is related to the NIC, and its entire definition is shown next. In this definition, the resource is configured with the dynamic private IP address and is associated with the previously defined subnet and the virtual network. Notice that no static IP address is supplied to this resource either through parameters or variables. It is this resource that we want to reconfigure with the static private IP, with the resource defined later in the template:

```
{
    "apiVersion": "2018-08-01",
    "type": "Microsoft.Network/networkInterfaces",
    "name": "[variables('nicName')]",
    "location": "[resourceGroup().location]",
    "dependsOn": [
      "[concat('Microsoft.Network/virtualNetworks/', variables('virtualNetworkName'))]"
    ],
    "properties": {
      "ipConfigurations": [
```

```
            {
              "name": "ipconfig1",
              "properties": {
                "privateIPAllocationMethod": "Dynamic",
                "subnet": {
                  "id": "[variables('subnetRef')]"
                }
              }
            }
          ]
        }
      },
```

The last resource in this template is the deployment resource that uses a nested template to reconfigure the dynamically assigned IP address to the static IP address. The definition of this resource is shown next. This resource has an inner template that by itself is a complete ARM template. This inner template redefines the previous NIC with the static IP address. There are a few important points to remember here.

First, the definition of the NIC in the inner template is the same as the previous NIC. The only difference is that instead of the dynamic IP address allocation method, it is static, and the static IP address is obtained by reading the runtime IP address allocated to the NIC during its first run. The rest of all the configuration of this resource is the same as the previous NIC, because we do not want to change any other property. However, if you want to change any properties of the NIC, it is possible to do so. For example, if you want to add a public IP address while reconfiguring, it is possible to do so.

Second, the deployment resource is dependent on the NIC resource. This means that the deployment resource should execute only after the execution of the first NIC resource. This is necessary, because we do not want to reconfigure a resource that is not yet created.

Third, the name of the NIC resource in an inner template is the same as that of the first NIC, although they both are defined within the same ARM template:

```
      {
            "apiVersion": "2018-01-01",
            "name": "nestedTemplate",
            "type": "Microsoft.Resources/deployments",
            "dependsOn": [
               "[concat('Microsoft.Network/networkInterfaces/',
      variables('nicName'))]"
            ],
            "properties": {
               "mode": "Incremental",
               "template": {
                  "$schema":
```

Design Patterns

```json
"https://schema.management.azure.com/schemas/2015-01-01/deploymentTemplate.json#",
    "contentVersion": "1.0.0.0",
    "resources": [
      {
        "apiVersion": "2015-06-15",
        "type": "Microsoft.Network/networkInterfaces",
        "name": "[variables('nicName')]",
        "location": "[resourceGroup().location]",
        "properties": {
          "ipConfigurations": [
            {
              "name": "ipconfig1",
              "properties": {
                "privateIPAllocationMethod": "static",
                "privateIPAddress": "[reference(variables('nicName')).ipConfigurations[0].properties.privateIPAddress]",
                "subnet": {
                  "id": "[variables('subnetRef')]"
                }
              }
            }
          ]
        }
      }
    ]
  }
}
```

Now, if you navigate to the NIC in Azure portal, you will notice that the IP address is static. The next screenshot shows the same:

Summary

This chapter focused on creating solutions, using the ARM template for known problems. Specific design patterns were used in this chapter to solve problems related to the reusability of ARM templates, creating multiple resources at the same time, dependencies among resources, the reconfiguring of existing resources from the same ARM template, tagging, the reuse of runtime values in the ARM template, and more. This chapter also focused on the decomposition of large ARM templates into smaller ARM templates, for higher reusability and modularity.

The next chapter is the last chapter of the book, and it will focus on the best practices related to the creation and deployment of the ARM templates.

8
ARM Template Best Practices

This is the last chapter of the book, and we have been writing **Azure Resource Manager** (**ARM**) templates throughout this book. You've probably noticed that there are multiple ways to write resources, parameters, and variables in an ARM template. Writing an ARM template that provisions an environment is easy; however, writing an ARM template that is also maintainable, readable, and easy to change is not. In the last chapter, we took a look at the topic of design patterns and how they help with creating maintainable ARM templates. Apart from design patterns, we should also follow certain best practices while authoring ARM templates. These best practices will ensure that ARM templates can be maintained, reused, and evolve easily over a period of time.

Some of the important best practices that should be implemented in every ARM template include the following:

- Best practices for security, such as using Azure Key vault
- Best Practices for declaring parameters and variables
- Deployment best practices
- Refrain from hard-coding values
- Commenting ARM templates

So, let's understand the best practices related to ARM templates.

Use resourceId function

The `resourceId` function generates resource identifiers that are well-formed, rather than via the manual concatenation of `string` values. There are no checks made while concatenating `string` variables, and a template will fail if there are any issues with the supplied values or the malformed `resourceId`. Instead, using `resourceId` will ensure that a proper resource identifier, including the subscription ID, resource group name, and resource information is generated. Using the `resourceId` function should be the preferred way of generating the resource identifier.

The next code statement in an ARM template builds a virtual machine resource identifier using string concatenation. This is a bad practice:

```
"[concat('/subscriptions/',subscription().subscriptionId,'/resourceGroups/'
,resourceGroup().name
,'/providers/','Microsoft.Compute/virtualMachines/',variables('vmName'))]"
```

Instead of using string concatenation, use `resourceId` to generate the resource identifier. The code shown next does the same thing as the previous code; however, it ensures that is it well-formed and less error-prone; this is a good practice:

```
resourceId('Microsoft.Compute/virtualMachines', variables('vmName'))
```

To generate a resource identifier for nested resources, similar code statement shown next can be used:

```
resourceId('Microsoft.SQL/servers/databases', parameters('sqlServerName'),
concat(parameters('sqlDatabaseName'))
```

The `resourceId` function takes the current subscription and resource group as default, parameter and they can be overridden by supplying values as parameters, as shown here:

```
resourceId('xxxxxxxx-xxxx-xxxx-
xxxxxxxxxxxx','resourcegroupname''Microsoft.SQL/servers/databases',
parameters('sqlServerName'), concat(parameters('sqlDatabaseName'))
```

Generate Resource Identifier used multiple times

Within an ARM template, there are times when a resource identifier is used multiple times in resource configurations. Instead of using the same code for generating a resource identifier multiple times, it is a good practice to generate them once within the variables section and use the variable in the resource configuration.

The `databaseIdentifier` and `subnetIdentifier` variables can be used at multiple places within the ARM template. The value is generated once and used multiple times. It also helps with maintenance, since making changes at a single place can affect operations in multiple places:

```
"variables": {

   "virtualNetworkName": "testvirtualNetwork",
```

```
    "subnetName": "testSubnetName",
    "databaseIdentifier": "[resourceId('Microsoft.SQL/servers/databases',
parameters('sqlServerName'), concat(parameters('sqlDatabaseName')))]",

    "subnetIdentifier":
"[resourceId('Microsoft.Network/virtualNetworks/subnets',
variables('virtualNetworkName'), variables('subnetName'))]"
    },
```

Use Comments

All parameters and resources should have comments associated with them. Comments help in understanding their purpose and usage. The purpose and the usage of the parameter and the resource should be easily understood by anyone reading the ARM template code. Comments in ARM templates are provided by means of the `metadata` element.

Both the `primaryServiceBusNamespaceName` and `primaryServiceBusSku` parameters have an addition `metadata` element. This element helps in adding comments within ARM templates:

```
    "parameters": {
      "primaryServiceBusNamespaceName": {
        "type": "string",
        "metadata": {
          "description": "Service Bus namespace name"
        }
      },

      "primaryServiceBusSku": {
        "type": "string",
        "metadata": {
          "description": "Service bus SKU"
        }
      },
```

Apart from Parameters, even Resources can have `metadata` element. This is shown in the following code block:

```
      {
        "apiVersion": "2017-04-01",
        "name": "[parameters('primaryServiceBusNamespaceName')]",
        "type": "Microsoft.ServiceBus/namespaces",
        "location": "[resourceGroup().location]",
        "metadata": {
          "description": "Service Bus namespace name"
```

```
        },
        "sku": {
          "name": "[parameters('primaryServiceBusSku')]"
        }
    },
```

Use Tags for resources and resource groups

Tags are important for the categorization of resources. It becomes extremely easy to generate focused reports based on these tags. Tags should be assigned to resources based on your requirements for reports. If you want to generate reports based on department or environments, they should be added as tags. Tags can help report the cost and the usage of Azure's resources as well.

Tags can be added to resources and resource groups. To add a tag to a resource in an ARM template, the `tags` element is used, and they can accept values from both variables and parameters. The next example shows the usage of tags within a resource definition:

```
        "tags": {
          "displayName": "SqlServer",
          "environmentName": "[parameters('environmentName')]",
          "Department":   "[variables('departmentName')]"
        },
```

Use parameters sparingly

There is a general tendency to add a parameter to every property related to resource configuration. Although it makes the template highly generic, it comes with a cost. ARM templates do not have many features for validating an incoming parameter. An ARM template can conduct basic checks in terms of the length of the parameter and whether or not it is mandatory. The users will not always know the appropriate values for some of these parameters.

Parameters should be defined only for those configurations that affect the size of the environment, the types of resources created, the cost of the environment, security-related information, and data that is needed to configure the resources.

As an example of the parameters for the environment size, we can have a `Large`, `Medium`, or `Small` environment. Based on the value, the appropriate SKU and the size of a resource should be provisioned. Users should not send `S2` as an SKU for creating a SQL Server database. A Small database should provision an `S2` SKU Azure database. A small environment might refer to three virtual machines, and a large one might provision 10 virtual machines. This is also known as **T-shirt sizing**.

An example of parameters that decide on the type of resource to provision could be Linux versus Windows Operating System or between Azure Service Bus Queues versus Azure Service Bus Topics.

Examples of the security-related parameter can include a user name and password information.

Examples of resource-specific configuration parameters can include the size of a virtual machine or the subnet it should be attached to.

Group related parameters

Again, it is a general tendency to declare many parameters for a resource configuration, and these parameters are put randomly within the parameters section. Ideally, the parameters for a resource configuration should be grouped together as a single parameter and sent to the ARM template.

In this example, an ARM template accepts a single SQL Server resource configuration parameter of the `object` data type:

```
"sqlServerProperties": {
  "type": "object"
},
```

And the parameters file provides all the parameters to it as a single object, as shown next:

```
"sqlServerProperties": {
  "value": {
    "administratorLogin": "eCommerceAdmin",
    "databaseName": "eCommerceDatabase",
    "collation": "SQL_Latin1_General_CP1_CI_AS",
    "edition": "Standard",
    "maxSizeBytes": "1073741824",
    "requestedServiceObjectiveName": "S0",
    "sqlserverName": "armtemplatebooksqlserver",
    "keyVaultName": "keyvaultarmtemplatebook",
    "keyVaultResourceGroupName": "ARMPatterns",
```

```
            "adminstratorPasswordSecretName": "adminstratorPasswordSQL"
        }
    },
```

Order parameters alphabetically

Ordering the parameter declaration alphabetically helps with identifying and navigating the parameter easily for anyone who is reading it.

The net parameter declaration in the ARM template shows that all the parameters are declared in alphabetical order, preferably in ascending order. Notice that the names of the parameter start with a and move toward z:

```
"parameters": {
  "appServicesInfo": {
    "type": "object"
  },

  "diagnosticlevel": {
    "type": "string"
  },
  "resourceGroupInfo": {
    "type": "array"
  },
  "sqlServerProperties": {
    "type": "object"
  },
  "storagekey": {
    "type": "securestring"
  },
  "TagsInfo": {
    "type": "object"
  }
}
```

Constraint parameters if possible

Parameters should be constrained as much as possible. Parameters provide additional elements such as `minValue`, `MaxValue`, `minLength`, `MaxLength`, and `allowedValues` and they should be used to validate the incoming parameter's value.

It is to be noted that these additional elements can only be used with parameters with `int`, `string`, and `array` data types. This means they cannot be used with objects data type.

The next code block shows examples of parameters using `minValue`, `MaxValue`, `minLength`, `MaxLength`, and `allowedValues` elements:

```
"parameters": {
   "environmentName": {
     "type": "string",
     "allowedValues": [ "DEV", "TST", "PRD", "SIT", "PAT", "STG", "UAT" ]
   },

   "department": {
     "type": "string",
     "maxLength": 30,
     "minLength": 5
   },

   "storageArray": {
     "type": "array",
     "maxLength": 5,
     "minLength": 2
   },

   "countofVirtualMachines": {
     "type": "int",
     "minValue": 2,
     "maxValue": 5
   }
}
```

Parameter's defaultValue and API versions

Use `defaultValue` property sparingly—it is not a good practice to use default values for parameters that do not need default values. Default values make supplying a value to the parameter optional. It is better to use variables for defining default values.

API versions are used for every resource configured in the ARM template. API versions should be statically defined within the resource configuration. Moreover, there are multiple API versions available for each resource. It is important to use the right API version for your requirements.

An API version's value should not be defined as part of the parameters declaration, nor is it recommended to put them in variables.

ARM Template Best Practices

The next code example shows that the `Microsoft.Sql/servers` resource is using an API of the 2017-10-01-preview version, although other versions, such as 2017-03-01-preview and 2014-04-01, are available:

```
{
     "type": "Microsoft.Sql/servers",
     "kind": "v12.0",
     "name": "[parameters('sqlServerName')]",
     "location": "[resourceGroup().location]",
     "apiVersion": "2017-10-01-preview",
     "properties": {
       "administratorLogin":
"[parameters('sqlServerAdministratorLoginName')]",
       "administratorLoginPassword":
"[parameters('sqlServerAdministratorLoginPassword')]",

       "version": "12.0"
     }
}
```

Declare All Resources as top-level resources

Although most of the resources are declared as top-level resources within the resources section of ARM templates, there are resources that are child resources of these top-level resources and declared within them. Examples of such child resources include the `databases` resource within the `Microsoft.Sql/servers` resource. The typical implementation of declaring the child resource within the parent resource is shown next:

```
{
     "name": "[variables('sqlserverName')]",
     "type": "Microsoft.Sql/servers",
     "location": "[parameters('location')]",
     "tags": {
       "displayName": "SqlServer"
     },
     "apiVersion": "2014-04-01",
     "properties": {
       "administratorLogin": "[parameters('sqlAdministratorLogin')]",
       "administratorLoginPassword":
"[parameters('sqlAdministratorLoginPassword')]",
       "version": "12.0"
     },
     "resources": [
```

```
        {
          "name": "[variables('databaseName')]",
          "type": "databases",
          "location": "[parameters('location')]",
          "tags": {
            "displayName": "Database"
          },
          "apiVersion": "2015-01-01",
          "dependsOn": [
            "[variables('sqlserverName')]"
          ],
          "properties": {
            "edition": "Basic",
            "collation": "SQL_Latin1_General_CP1_CI_AS",
            "maxSizeBytes": "1073741824",
            "requestedServiceObjectiveName": "Basic"
          }
        }
      ]
    }
```

One of the limitations of such a practice is that child resources cannot use the copy-and-looping feature provided by ARM templates. If you need to create multiple instances of a child resource based on a requirement or in the future, these child resources should be defined as top-level resources alongside their parent resources. However, a relationship between the parent resource and the child resource should still be maintained by way of naming the resource and resource type. This is shown in the following code listing, and it is a best practice.

First, we define the parent resource, `Microsoft.Sql/servers`, as shown here:

```
    {
        "type": "Microsoft.Sql/servers",
        "kind": "v12.0",
        "name": "[parameters('sqlServerName')]",
        "location": "[resourceGroup().location]",
        "apiVersion": "2017-10-01-preview",
        "properties": {
          "administratorLogin":
"[parameters('sqlServerAdministratorLoginName')]",
          "administratorLoginPassword":
"[parameters('sqlServerAdministratorLoginPassword')]",
          "version": "12.0"
        }
    },
```

Then the child resource `databases` is defined at the same level as the parent resource. Notice the `type` and `name` properties for this resource. The type is no longer just `databases`. It is qualified with the `Microsoft.Sql/servers/databases` parent resource type, and the name of the resource also consists of the parent resource name separated using a forward slash (/). Notice how the `copy` element is used to create multiple database instances:

```
{
        "type": "Microsoft.Sql/servers/databases",
        "name": "[concat(parameters('sqlServerName'),'/',parameters('sqlDatabaseName'),copyIndex())]",
        "location": "[resourceGroup().location]",
        "apiVersion": "2017-10-01-preview",
        "dependsOn": [
          "[parameters('sqlServerName')]"
        ],
        "copy": {
          "name": "alldatabases",
          "count": 2
        },
        "properties": {
          "edition": "[parameters('sqlDatabaseEdition')]",
          "collation": "[parameters('sqlDatabaseCollation')]",
          "maxSizeBytes": "[parameters('sqlDatabaseMaxSizeBytes')]",
          "requestedServiceObjectiveName": "[parameters('sqlDatabaseRequestedServiceObjectiveName')]"
        }
      }
```

Output Resource Properties and Configuration

It is a good practice to output results from ARM templates using the `Outputs` section. Outputs are important because they provide additional feedback to the deployer in terms of a resource's status and its configuration. This output configuration information can then further be used for sending the same template to other resources, or it can be used in other templates. These outputs can also be used to unit test the resource configuration using **Pester**.

An example of an ARM template generating outputs and returning values is shown next. Here, two values are returned—one of them is of the type `string` and returns the FQDN of the created Azure SQL Server, and the other is of the type `object`, returning the complete Azure Server configuration:

```
"outputs": {
    "SQLServer1": {
        "type": "string",
        "value": "[reference(parameters('sqlServerProperties').sqlserverName).fullyQualifiedDomainName]"
    },

    "SQLServer": {
        "type": "object",
        "value": "[reference(parameters('sqlServerProperties').sqlserverName)]"
    }
}
```

Resource-naming conventions

Each resource provisioned using the ARM template should be named consistently using a particular naming convention. The naming convention should be developed within the organization. These names should be generated within the variables section, as shown in the following code block:

```
"multiLocation": {
    "copy": [
        {
            "name": "location",
            "count": "[length(parameters('resourceGroupInfo'))]",
            "input": {
                "resourceGroupName": "[concat('RGP','-',parameters('environmentName'),'-',parameters('resourceGroupInfo')[copyIndex('location')].resourceGroupName)]",
                "appServicePlanName": "[toLower(concat('asp','-',parameters('resourceGroupInfo')[copyIndex('location')].resourceGroupSuffix,'-',parameters('appServicePlanSkuName'),'-',parameters('environmentName')))]",
                "webAppName": "[toLower(concat('web','-',parameters('resourceGroupInfo')[copyIndex('location')].resourceGroupSuffix,'-', parameters('appServicePlanSkuName'),'-',parameters('environmentName')))]"
```

                }
            }
        ]
    }

Storage of Linked templates

All linked templates should be stored in a well-defined blob storage account, within containers secured by an SAS token. Linked templates should generate outputs that can be used by a parent template.

Resource Dependencies

The dependencies among resources should be acyclical rather than cyclical. This means it should not be possible to return to the same resource from multiple resources. The previous `Chapter 7`, *Design Patterns* described patterns that can be used to design dependencies among resources.

Using Key Vaults for secrets

Key Vaults should be used to store secrets, credentials, and keys. There should not be any secrets, credentials, and keys visible in either an ARM template or its parameters file. The previous chapter on design patterns shows two different ways to use Azure Key Vaults for the storage and usage of secrets.

Using ContentVersion

Change the `ContentVersion` of ARM templates if there are bug fixes that introduced breaking changes, or while adding or removing parameters.

Deployment – Best Practices

Azure provides multiple ways to deploy ARM templates. An ARM template could be deployed using PowerShell, Azure CLI, Azure-provided SDKs, REST APIs, and even through the Azure portal:

- **Validate template**: While using PowerShell, it is important to validate the template before deploying the template. Azure PowerShell provides the `Test-AzureRmResourceGroupDeployment` cmdlet for this purpose. It takes the path to the template file and the optional parameters file, to check whether the template is well formed and that it does not contain errors. This cmdlet does not generate a new deployment in Azure.
- **Unique deployment name**: Azure provides the `New-AzureRmResourceGroupDeployment` cmdlet for deploying an ARM template. This command takes the name of the deployment as its parameter. This name should be unique for easy identification on the portal and for auditing purposes.
- **Deployment with Verbose output**: The `New-AzureRmResourceGroupDeployment` cmdlet should be deployed using the verbose switch to get detailed information about the deployment.
- **Using ARM template functions**: ARM templates provide numerous functions that can be used with expressions. These functions should be used in appropriate situations.
- **Empty function**: Use the empty function to check whether there is any value within a parameter or a variable. It can be applied to `array`, `string`, and `object` data types.
- **URI function**: Use the URI function to generate URLs, instead of concatenating them using the `concat` function.
- **Verbose and Debug option**: Use the `verbose` and `debug` PowerShell options while deploying the template. They provide additional information that helps with troubleshooting and the diagnostics of ARM templates.

Summary

This chapter is the last chapter of the book, and it focuses on using best practices while developing ARM templates. It is very easy to create ARM templates, but this can become very difficult to change and maintain. These best practices help with creating ARM templates that are easy to change and maintain. There are best practices related to variables, parameters, resources, security, outputs, and deployment. These were discussed within this chapter extensively, and readers are advised to use these best practices whenever creating or reviewing an ARM template.

Best of luck, happy learning, and keep authoring ARM templates!

Other Books You May Enjoy

If you enjoyed this book, you may be interested in these other books by Packt:

Hands-On Azure for Developers
Kamil Mrzygłód

ISBN: 9781789340624

- Implement serverless components such as Azure functions and logic apps
- Integrate applications with available storages and containers
- Understand messaging components, including Azure Event Hubs and Azure Queue Storage
- Gain an understanding of Application Insights and other proper monitoring solutions
- Store your data with services such as Azure SQL and Azure Data Lake Storage
- Develop fast and scalable cloud applications

Implementing Azure Solutions - Second Edition
Florian Klaffenbach

ISBN: 9781789343045

- Create and manage a Kubernetes cluster in Azure Kubernetes Service (AKS)
- Implement site-to-site VPN and ExpressRoute connections in your environment
- Explore the best practices in building and deploying app services
- Use Telemetry to monitor your Azure Solutions
- Design an Azure IoT solution and learn how to operate in different scenarios
- Implement a Hybrid Azure Design using Azure Stack

Leave a review - let other readers know what you think

Please share your thoughts on this book with others by leaving a review on the site that you bought it from. If you purchased the book from Amazon, please leave us an honest review on this book's Amazon page. This is vital so that other potential readers can see and use your unbiased opinion to make purchasing decisions, we can understand what our customers think about our products, and our authors can see your feedback on the title that they have worked with Packt to create. It will only take a few minutes of your time, but is valuable to other potential customers, our authors, and Packt. Thank you!

Index

A

advanced deployments
  about 101
  copy, using with deployment resources 102
  deployment resource, used for deploying resources into multiple resource groups 104, 106, 107, 109
  nested deployments 112, 113
  resource groups, creating with ARM templates 103
  resources, deploying into multiple resource group in multiple subscriptions 110
API version 55, 207
app service plan template 175
ARM templates, best practices
  API versions 207
  comments 203
  constraint parameters 207
  ContentVersion, using 212
  defaultValue, using sparingly 207
  dependency, among resources 212
  Key Vaults, using for secrets 212
  linked template storage 212
  objects, outputting 210
  parameter declaration, ordering alphabetically 206
  parameters, using sparingly 204
  related parameters, grouping 205
  resource identifier, generating for multiple usage 202
  resource naming convention 211
  resource properties, outputting 210
  resourceId function 201, 202
  resources, declaring as top-level resources 208, 209
  tags, using for resource groups 204
  tags, using for resources 204

ARM templates
  about 13
  benefits 13
  Complete deployment 43
  complete template 60
  conditions 97, 98, 99, 100
  contentVersion 30
  dependencies, between resources 188, 189
  dependsOn 64, 65, 67
  deploying 170, 171
  deploying, Azure CLI used 39, 40
  deploying, Azure portal used 36, 37, 38
  deploying, PowerShell used 40, 41
  deploying, ways 35
  deployment, best practices 213
  designing, process 13, 14, 15
  expressions 52, 53
  functions 53
  Incremental deployment 43
  multiple resources, creating in loop 190
  outputs 30
  outputs, retrieving from 148
  parameters 30, 44, 45
  parameters, grouping 47
  parameters, referencing 46
  reference function 67, 68, 69, 70, 72
  resourceId 72, 73, 75
  resources 30, 54
  resources, nesting 61, 63
  resources, tagging 192
  runtime sharing, of property values 193
  schema 29
  SecureObject 17
  SecureString 17
  structure 29
  technical prerequisites 163
  unit testing 142, 144, 145, 146, 148

used, for creating resource groups 103
  variables 30
  writing 31, 32, 33, 35
assertions, Pester
  reference 150
Azure App Services template 176, 177, 179, 181
Azure CLI
  used, for deploying templates 39, 40
Azure portal
  used, for deploying templates 36, 37, 38
Azure PowerShell modules
  download link 28
Azure Resource Manager API component 18
Azure Resource Manager
  about 17
  governance 22
  management 19
  monitoring 21
  provisioning 17
Azure SQL template 173, 174

C

comments
  in ARM templates 203
conditions, ARM templates 97, 98, 99, 100
configuration data, DSC
  using 137, 138, 140
configuration management 10
configuration templates 161
configuration
  inside, Azure virtual machine 120, 121, 122, 123
constructs 44
ContentVersion
  using 212
copy
  used, for generating multiple variables 94, 95, 96
CustomScriptExtension
  as separate resource 129
  output, obtaining from 131
  using, with Linux virtual machines 132

D

defaultValue
  using, sparingly 207
dependsOn, ARM templates 64
deployment best practices, ARM templates 213
deployment resource
  resources, deploying into multiple resource groups 104, 106, 107, 109
desired state configuration (DSC) 134, 135, 136
development environment
  setting up 26
  Visual Studio 2017, using as 26, 27
  Visual Studio Code, using as 28

E

expressions, ARM templates 52, 53

F

functions, ARM templates 53

G

generalized templates 172
governance, Azure Resource Manager
  about 22
  locks 23
  policies 22
  role-based access control (RBAC) 22

H

hosting plan 65

I

Infrastructure as Code 11, 12
intermediate templates 160, 161

J

JavaScript Object Notation (JSON) 15
JSON value
  arrays 17
  Boolean 16
  null 16
  numbers 16
  objects 17

strings 16

K

Key Vault information
  dynamic declaration 186, 188
  static usage 183, 184, 185
Key Vault
  using, for passwords 183
  using, for secrets 183, 212
known configuration templates 160, 161

L

linked template storage 212
linked templates
  implementing 76, 77, 78, 80, 81, 82
  using 75, 76
Linux virtual machines
  CustomScriptExtension, using with 132

M

management, Azure Resource Manager
  about 19
  hierarchical 20
  resource groups 20
  tags 20
master ARM template
  deploying 169
modular ARM templates
  about 172
  app service plan template 175
  Azure App Services template 176, 177, 179, 181
  Azure SQL template 173, 174
  generalized templates 172
  need for 159
  scenario 162
monitoring, Azure Resource Manager
  about 21
  actions 21
  alerts 21
  logs 21
multiple instances
  creating, of resource property 92, 93
  creating, of resource type 88, 89, 91
multiple variables

generating, copy used 94, 95, 96

N

nested deployments
  creating 112, 113
nested templates 83, 84, 85
Network Interface Card (NIC) 145

O

objects
  outputting 211
outputs
  retrieving, from ARM templates 148

P

parameters
  about 44
  grouping 205
  in ARM templates 44, 45
  referencing, within template 46
  using, sparingly 204
Pester
  about 210
  using 150
PowerShell
  used, for deploying templates 40, 41
protectedSettings
  using 127
provisioning, Azure Resource Manager
  about 17
  API-driven 19
  automation 19
  multi-region 19
  parallel 19

R

references
  in ARM templates 67, 69, 70, 72
resource groups
  creating, ARM templates used 103
  tags, using for 204
resource identifier
  generating 202
resource naming convention, ARM template 211

resource properties
  multiple instances, creating of 92, 93
  outputting 210
resource provider 55
resource type
  multiple instances, creating of 88, 89, 91
resourceId function 201, 202
resourceId, ARM templates 72, 73, 75
resources, ARM templates
  about 54
  locations 58, 59
  names 54
  nested resources 55, 56, 57
  outputs 59
  properties 57
  types 55
resources
  redefining, in same template 194, 195, 196, 197
  tags, using for 204
role definition 22
role-based access control (RBAC) 22

S

SAS tokens
  used, for protecting scripts 125, 126, 127
scripts
  protecting, SAS tokens used 125, 126, 127
Secure Access Signatures (SAS) 77
Serial mode
  multiple instances, creating of resource type 91
Single Responsibility Principle 160
SKUs 161

T

T-shirt sizing 161, 205
tags
  using, for resource groups 204
  using, for resources 204
technical prerequisites, ARM templates

  about 163
  ARM templates, uploading to storage 165
  Azure AD service principle, creating 168
  Azure Key Vault, creating 166
  Azure login setup 163
  Azure Storage Account, creating 164
  Azure Storage blob container, creating 164
  Azure Storage SAS token, generating 165
  Azure subscription setup 163
  new resource group 163
  permissions, assigning to service principle 169
  secrets, creating in Key Vault 167
template patterns
  about 171
  modular ARM templates 172
test harness setup
  about 151
  complete unit test script 156
  NIC, unit testing 153, 154
  public IP address, unit testing 152
  storage account, unit testing 152
  virtual machine, unit testing 155, 156
  virtual networks, unit testing 153

U

unit testing
  about 141, 142
  ARM templates 142, 144, 145, 146, 148

V

variables
  about 48
  accessing 49
Visual Studio 2017
  using, as development environment 26, 27
Visual Studio Code
  using, as development environment 28
Visual Studio
  download link 26